Farewell
Performance

the Collected
Later Poems
of Vernon Scannell

Farewell Performance
the Collected Later Poems of Vernon Scannell

edited by Martin Reed
and Jeremy Robson

Smoke
STACK
BOOKS

Smokestack Books
1 Lake Terrace, Grewelthorpe,
Ripon HG4 3BU
e-mail: info@smokestack-books.co.uk
www.smokestack-books.co.uk

ISBN 9781838465339

Smokestack Books
is represented by
Inpress Ltd

for Jo Peters

Contents

Of Love and War

Behind the Lines

Preface

With the publication of *Collected Poems 1950–1993* (Robson Books, 1993) Vernon Scannell felt he had brought together the best of what he had written and, in his usual self-deprecating way, doubted there would be much more to follow.

How fortunate we are that he was so mistaken and that, in his final fourteen years, he produced four outstanding major collections: *The Black and White Days* (Robson Books, 1996), *Views and Distances* (Enitharmon, 2000), *Of Love and War* (Robson Books, 2002) and *Behind the Lines* (Shoestring Press, 2004) and two smaller collections, *A Place to Live* (The Happy Dragons' Press, 2007) and *Last Post* (Shoestring Press, 2007). All of these collections are presented here in full with the exception of some pieces from *Of Love and War* which can be found in the 1993 *Collected*. Thanks are due to the original publishers for permission to reproduce the poems.

Vernon also wrote work for younger readers, much of which is far too good to be age-limited, and a representative sample is included in the final section, Uncollected Poems, together with three final poems written at the very end of his life.

Far from completing the story in 1993, Vernon continued to write with incisiveness and humanity, poems which reflect, as he put it in his introduction to the 1993 *Collected Poems*, 'a real need to explore and articulate experiences which have been important to me.' To the end of his life, he reflected unflinchingly on his own experience of love, war, cancer and old age as well as on a huge variety of other matters. As the reader of this collection will discover, his customary wry wit and good humour, allied to a formidable mastery of poetic technique, never deserted him.

The original *Collected Poems 1950–1993* is now published by Faber. With the arrival of this *Later Collected*, in the centenary year of Vernon Scannell's birth, all the poems he wished to preserve are in print and I hope they will reach many new readers as well as those who already cherish his work.

Martin Reed

Introduction

Simply turning the manuscript pages of the poems that make up this fascinating collection provided for one reader, and probably many others of his generation and younger, a vivid and touching reminder of the loss to poetry when Vernon Scannell died in 2007.

I was hearing again and again the clear, gently authoritative, voice in which he delivered late poems like these and, over many years, a wealth of earlier work produced in a long and diverse career. He continued to give readings as long as he was able, which in his case was into his early 80s, and at that final stage he was still writing with the old, undiminished determination – and as prolifically as ever – still a compelling solo performer or else one of a group or team of poets alongside colleagues mostly much younger than himself.

The venue could be a school or college, a public library or lecture hall, a noisy urban pub or a quiet country retreat given over to creative writing courses. Vernon was at ease in any of them and audiences of all ages welcomed him with a blend of affection and high respect.

This is not to suggest that Vernon Scannell deserves to be remembered principally for memorable presentations of his poetry. On the page, as will be evident from this volume, his poems are as impressive for their quality and their accessibility for the reader as he made them sound from the platform. In the end this collection deserves to be read for the reason that many of the poems are among his best and ought to be acknowledged as a remarkable conclusion to a lifetime of creative effort.

He returns here to almost all of his favourite subjects: love and its vicissitudes, war and its aftermaths in his painful memories of it, time and ageing, place and its resonance for him, the challenges that life throws at him and his ways of coping with them. To begin with love: he was rarely a poet of romantic love in the conventional sense of exploring and/or indulging an unrequited emotion. He was much more a poet of passion spurned and ending in frustration or disillusion. In one brief piece an emperor's beautiful daughter counts 'hapless suitors' like sheep trailing past her as she drops off to sleep. Yet equally moving – and appealingly sensible – are poems which implicitly rejoice in love as something from which he has derived lasting reassurance and benefit over long periods of time.

The experience of war retained its place in Vernon's poetry to the end, his long life guaranteeing that no part of it that had left any important impression on him was neglected. He registers the bitter irony of the death that more than once comes altogether unexpectedly to those who seem destined in the short term to be guaranteed survival. 'Robbie' in the *Of Love and War* sequence being an example. Anything resembling an explosion, and certainly any gun-like sound is, despite the fact that it is heard decades later, immediately taken to be the sound of a bombardment occurring somewhere distant.

Occasionally, though, war returns to him in the form of a vivid personal moment in the conflict, an incident which hardly any other poet has registered with equivalent detail. 'Final Run' shows a remarkable ability to summon up the atmosphere inside a bomber engaged in an air-raid, the 'perspex world' in which crew members exchange terse messages while pursued by German fighters (Messerschmitts and Junkers); or the utterly different character of the world away from the battlefield in 'Behind the Lines', in a place where 'distance tames the menace of the guns', but all the same the sense of danger is undiminished and poetry has been 'abandoned in despair'. Altogether extraordinary is his account of a punishment for tank commanders refusing to take charge of another crew when the first had died in battle:

> You'll be confined in darkness and we'll not
> Allow you more than two hours' light each day.

'Compulsory Mourning' is the description given by the title of this poem, and readers might be surprised to find that Vernon couched his narrative here in fast-flowing rhyming couplets, almost as if there had been a lighter side to it:

> I think that this will concentrate the mind
> Quite wonderfully, as Doctor Johnson said.
> In there you'll find a way to mourn your dead.

The passing of time has done little or nothing to reduce the pain of having had to live through the experience of war and suffer frightening memories of it which return decades later. In many places here he is preoccupied with language and the way it has changed while he has been a writer. In the poem called 'Words' he appreciates the oddity in the fact that being 'shit-scared' in the past is now a case of suffering from 'pre-traumatic stress disorder'.

Alongside impressive additions of distressingly real and previously unexplored material to the body of his work is a number of poems of a formal kind which his admirers will expect, part of his appeal having always been in the importance he attaches to shape and form in poetry. He believed readers would agree with him if his work took on, whatever subject he was engaged with, a traditional appearance. It was desirable, though never compulsory, for poems to contain rhyme and to offer discernible rhythmic effects. Sometimes he can be boldly setting out to impress with a villanelle (or with that lengthy exercise in couplets).

But the most frequent example of adherence to common notions of what poetry is is the 14-line span of the pieces here which are sonnets, or might count as sonnets, giving him a form that allows contrasting treatments of a range of subjects. Effete figures from the 1890s become the victims of sharp satire in 'Fin de Siècle'. Rueful dark comedy is the fate of 'those lovely girls we used to know' in 'Changing Roles'; 'Storm Poem' re-examines a favourite topic for him, the way in which a poem as 'a thing of magic and mesmeric force', can dismally lose its hold on him between night and morning. This is the common experience of many, perhaps even most, poets, and Vernon Scannell returns so frequently to it that a reader might begin to expect a poem to show signs of weakening. Never the case. The two shortish concluding sections here, *A Place to Live* and *Last Post,* both of which appeared in the year he died, commanded and satisfied his readership with their strength and energy, even when the mood was inherently gloomy and he has despaired of seeing in his time 'a taste for shapeliness, cool argument and melody's fulfilment' ever coming back.

Alan Brownjohn

The Black
and White
Days

The First Piano on the Moon

has not been launched as yet, but it could be.
It's not past human ingenuity
to anchor it on some bleak lunar sea.
The vision and intelligence of man
has not shown evidence more powerful than
the presence of the thing itself, which can
be marvelled at for what it does yet seen
not only as a wonderful machine
but as aesthetic object. It could stand
in frozen silence and be no less grand.

Of course, like every dazzling artefact,
it did not suddenly appear intact
but it evolved; the simple dulcimer
was probably its earliest ancestor.
To me, more magical than *Gemini 8*
or Russian *Soyuz 10*, its intricate
fine mechanism: damper, check and spring,
the wires and pivot-point, everything
concealed behind dark gleam of wood in which
the keys lie white as milk and black as pitch.

So dream of it, lid lifted to beguile
a future astronaut with its fixed smile.
Quite possible, by then, he would not know
what purpose this device once served, although
he'd never doubt that it was made by man,
but hardly guess that parts of it began
as bits of mammoth and its habitat,
nor, in that sterile silence, realise that,
held in this graceful engine's wooden chest,
chained, sonic constellations, glittering, rest.

Elgar Louts

Their favourite season is autumn
When the Malverns seem to shift
Slightly sideways in the morning mist
And the chill of the wind
Is tempered by a breath
Of leafmeal's sweet decay.

This is when they come
Cavorting down the slopes
Waving their Union Jacks, their eyes
Gleaming, moist, as if each sees
Visions of white cenotaphs
And sacrificial deeds.

In the village inn they raise
Their tankards and drink deep
To yellowing memories
Of bugle-calls and battlefields
And swear that they can hear
The far off thunder of the guns.

And later, after dark, before
The final call of time
When everyone's at least half-pissed
They weep like candles for the lost
And golden girl, that drift of hair
In cello-light, the secret smile.

Bare arms and shoulders, fluent, white;
Thoughtful fingers coaxing sighs
And soft melodious moans from strings;
All the gleam and glimmer gone
With Olaf and Caractacus
And the Worcester Asylum Band.

Fin de Siècle

All handsome or, at least, they have their charm,
A college elegance, insouciant grace;
They lounge on pampered turf and every face
Is smiling, dreamily perhaps, quite calm,
Oblivious of any lurking harm.
In light like lemonade each takes his place,
And knows he owns far more than that small space,
Unruffled by the slightest doubt or qualm.

Before the darkness falls they must decide
Exactly where their marvellous talents lie –
Poet, statesman, wit or spiritual guide –
Though none can prophesy or try to cheat
The various ways that they will have to die
Of bravery, boredom or the spirochaete.

Magnum Opus

in memoriam Jacob Kramer 1892–1962

One night in The Victoria in Leeds
Jacob said to me, 'Before I die
I'm going to paint a picture that will stun
them all. They think I've lost
whatever talent I once had,
that drink and craziness have neutered me.
I'll prove them wrong.
It's going to be a northern landscape,
forests, mountains, peaks, a pitiless sky –
but non-specific, if you follow me –
a landscape of the heart.
It's haunted me for years.
I'll show you... look ...'

And on the surface of the bar
he slopped a little of his beer
and with one spatulate forefinger drew
the soaring outline of the mountain-range.

'And here,' he muttered, wheezing, 'down below
in darker tones are hooded figures,
or they could be trees, or both ... you see?'

I stared and for a spell-bound moment glimpsed
the apocalyptic vision Jacob saw.
And then the barman's damp and grimy cloth
came swishing down and wiped the lot away.
'Drink up now gents, it's way past time,' he said.
'I reckon all of us should be in bed.'

The Black and White Days

Not only dreams were shot in black and white
But all the wide-eyed world of day and night;
           The music, too,
As black and white as piano keyboard or
Bleached tuxes and black ties the band all wore,
           Whose each jet shoe
That tapped the ragtime out would always show
A small pale highlight gleaming on the toe,
           And you could tell
The Leader by the large carnation which,
Like a curled-up spider, black as pitch,
           Slept on his white lapel.

The hat-check girls in fishnet tights applied
Dark lipstick to their mouths that looked like dried
           Blood or paint
Against white skin and sugar-icing teeth;
The blonde-haired singer wore a tight black sheath
           From whose constraint
The smooth-as-candle flesh flowed out and swelled
In bosom, tapering arms, and hands that held
           Sad emptiness
As blues' slow lamentations drifted round
Her silver-haloed head, deep midnight sound
           Of smoky, sweet distress.

The days of black and white, of sniffed cocaine,
Black guns and hard-boiled shirt fronts shocked with stain
          Like spreading ink,
Black blood, small maps of doomed desires, and fears,
Mad loyalties, betrayals, kisses, tears,
          The molls in mink,
Mascara smeared; the sidewalks in the rain
Varnished by lamps that laid a silver chain,
          Reflected light,
Across black paving where the gangsters died.
And checkered concrete blocks soared up to hide
          Night skies from sight.

But surely those were shadows on a screen?
This multicoloured world has never been
          Like that at all.
Did not gold lights gush in, rich curtains close?
Well, yes, the anthem played and we all rose,
          Yet I recall,
As we filed slowly out on whispering feet
And reached the almost silent, city street,
          Where all the bars
And shops were dark and shut, we started back
Beneath a natural sky, nun's-habit black,
          Sprinkled with salt of stars.

Farewell Performance

Shuffle of shoes, scrape and creak, voices
Murmur, a woman laughs, then lights are doused
And darkness floods the hall and drowns all noise;
The platform and the piano, though, are hosed
With dazzling lather and the keyboard smiles.

It smiles and waits. The old man makes his entrance,
Moving slowly on uncertain feet,
A mobile hawthorn, gnarled and blackened, bent,
So slow we think he'll never reach his seat;
To him the walk must seem to cover miles.

And from the bright-lit platform a faint odour
Of sweet decay drifts in the staring air
As he attains the stool. He is so old
Applause might be for his arriving there.
His head is bowed so we can't see his eyes,

And if the ancient skull were turned towards us
Dark sockets might direct their empty gaze
From where he settles at the keyboard. Pause
Of taut anxiety before he plays,
Then apprehension melts, and pity dies.

We hear the Liszt sonata in B minor
Flow and ripple through compliant space
To work sly sorcery along the spine
And pierce the heart with that familiar grace
Of truth and love that brook no compromise.

His hands dance on the keys; the nimble fingers
Are young as they cavort, caress, compel
Involuntary surrender while they sing
Of bliss and melancholy, heaven and hell;
It is not their mortality we smell.

Dirigible

Summer of 1930 in Eccles:
An eight-year-old boy was bowling his hoop
On the cobbles, a rusty and spokeless rim
Of a bicycle wheel; it bounced and rattled
Down Bardsley Street between the dark rows
Of crouching houses. A buttercup sun
In a clean blue sky. The boy was on holiday.

He was alone in the street, but not for long:
Solitude burst in a gaping of doors,
Loud callings and laughter, a flutter of dusters,
Aprons and towels, a festival feeling,
Everyone pointing and peering skywards,
Hands shading eyes like peaks of caps.
The boy let his hoop fall with a clatter.

And he, like the others, stared upwards, his mouth
As wide as his eyes as he saw the thing come
High over the roofs, bumbling, benign,
An enormous prize marrow, lacquered with silver,
The sunlight slithering over its skin,
Those weightless tons floating, preposterous and beautiful:
'It's the R One Hundred and One!' cried a woman.

Now he could hear its five engines drumming
As it floated closer, at last loomed directly
Over their heads. It did not seem possible
That men had devised it, were even now watching
From seats in the gondola under its belly:
To the boy it was magical, a wingless marvel,
A skyborne leviathan floating on nothing.

He stayed in the street long after the wonder
Had passed out of sight and the other spectators
Were back in the unenchanted places,
The sunless sculleries of mangle and copper
And chores of any ordinary morning.
He stayed and he stared as if the blue heavens
Might still be embossed with a trace of its presence.

Weeks later, when summer had ripened and fallen
And evenings came early with sad smoky breath,
The news of disaster fluttered the leaves
In gutter and parlour; the boy saw the smudged
And desolate picture, the huge fallen creature,
Black skeleton of girders scattered and broken,
The silvery skin consumed by the flames.

It had crashed on a hillside in France. It would never
Rise from its ashes and ride high again
And shine in the skies of Eccles, although
A ghost of its body hung shimmering and pale
In the sky in the skull of the Bardsley Street boy,
Would stay there, impervious to time and to gravity,
Melding to myth that no flames could destroy.

Family Secret

An old man now,
He roots among the rubble in the dark
Where dusty images of childhood lurk
Observing how
They are uncovered by some sensuous whim,
A trick of evening light surprising him
Before soft slam of night,
Tobacco-wraith and candle-smoke,
The wistful aspiration of violin.

A sepia close-up:
His father's face with joke moustache, eyes meek
Yet mischievous beneath the cheeky peak
Of service-cap;
Killed in France before his child was born.
No picture of the mother. She had gone
Peculiar, they said,
And disappeared. She must be dead
And buried long ago, the grave not known.

That's how he came
To live with Grannie, Grandpa and, of course,
The two huge uncles in the gaslit house
In Cuthbert Lane.
So many shapes and shades, such fears and joys,
Sly ambiguities; the distant noise
Of no-man's-land was heard
Behind domestic chimes of chores,
Low grumble of big guns and bugle-calls.

One afternoon
Grannie, with the kettle, making tea,
Splashed some boiling water on his knee.
The scalding wound
Howled loud and, later, when the swollen hurt
Was dressed and eased, though sobs still sputtered out,
One of the uncles said,
'Be a brave soldier, lad!' The boy
Gulped back his tears: 'I will. Just like my Dad!'

The kitchen blinked.
It held its breath; the silence clamped down hard.
He felt as if he'd said a wicked word,
But could not think
What it could be. He knew that it was he
Who'd frozen every sound. Then suddenly
His Grannie laughed and tried
To sweep unease away, although
The boy still felt perturbed and mystified.

What they all knew
He feels they should have told him long ago
Before deluded pride and love had swollen so.
This much is true:
His Dad had been no hero but a child,
A frightened boy who'd sprawled face-down in mud
With no salutes, no wild
Or mournful bugle-calls, no flags,
But dawn's death-rattle of the firing-squad.

Compulsory Mourning

'M. described his treatment of tank commanders who had lost crews and were unwilling to command another tank as "compulsory mourning". He arranged for them "...to be confined to a small darkened room for three days with an order to mourn" and blunt statements were made about their selfishness... they were fed on water and bread alone and were allowed one hour's daylight and one hour's electric light a day.'
from a report on 'The Northfield Experiment', a survey of psychiatric treatment given to soldiers in Northfield Military Hospital, Birmingham 1940–47

I lie in darkness on this bed of stone.
The shrewd cold bites like acid to the bone
And I am sick with gelded rage and hate,
And something else I can't quite designate,
A bitter taste, like guilt. And then the flood
Of concentrated loathing, dark as blood,
Surges though me and it leaves behind,
Among the sludge and lumber in the mind,
An image, vast and vivid, of his face,
Plump, well-shaven, showing not a trace
Of doubt or sympathy, this man who claims
That he's not hoodwinked by my little games,
And sees with X-ray eyes through walls of bone
Inside the haunted skull, and he alone
Can teach me how to mourn as I should do
The charred and blackened things that were my crew.
I think of his soft hands, like pastry dough,
And how they'd spit and sizzle in the glow
Inside the turret of a brewed-up tank.

Yesterday he said, 'I'll be quite frank.
You men are selfish shits – I see you grin!
All you can think of is your precious skin!
Well I am here to bring you to your senses

And find a way to break through those defences
That you have built, no doubt unconsciously,
Against accepting what is clear to me:
To mourn your former crew would mean that you
Must face mortality as something true,
Not just the death of others, but your own.
You can't admit we all must die alone.
All right. I grant the treatment might appear
A little harsh, but let me make this clear:
It's not a punishment although it may,
To you, seem not so different, shall we say,
From doing Solitary at Aldershot.
You'll be confined in darkness and we'll not
Allow you more than two hours' light each day.
You'll be on bread and water. There you'll stay
For three full days and nights and we shall find,
I think, that this will concentrate the mind
Quite wonderfully, as Dr Johnson said.
In there you'll find a way to mourn your dead.'

And he, of course, is wrong as he could be.
The dead are dead and mean no more to me
Than I to them. Though wait! I must admit
There's something else to say, and this is it:
The dead can't smell themselves – at least I pray
To Christ they can't! How terrible if they
Not only have to bear, but be their smell
For evermore in some peculiar hell!
That smell is in my nostrils, seems to spread
Inside my mouth and throat, it's in my head.
And with it come the voices of the war,
The glint of pain and terror through the roar
Of our Crusader's engine and the shrill
Static, morse and jamming noise that spill
From radio to season this rich din;
And, from outside, the almost childish, thin
Rattle of machine guns and blunt thud
Of eighty-eights. And then the tune of blood,

A soft insistent note, a kind of sigh
That lingers when the other voices die
And is ubiquitous. It joins the scent
Of cooking human flesh, is redolent
Of war and all that means, and ever meant.

In my protracted night the hours are melled
Into a timeless slur and I am held
By links of frozen minutes to a stake
Of impotence and anger. Though awake
I can't escape the images and sounds
That rise from nightmare's heaving burial grounds.
But I'll survive. And, furthermore, *his* scorn
And punitive attempts to make me mourn
The cinders of my crew will never crack
This resolution never to go back
And do it all again. In just three days
I'll rise from here and walk into the blaze
Of morning sunshine like the third day lad,
The Son of Man, and I shall swear I've had
A change of heart, that now my single aim
Is vengeance on the swine who are to blame
For my dead comrades' fate. Then he will claim
A medical and military success,
And he'll be wrong again. My readiness
To soldier on will be a trickster's act,
But he'll be fooled and swallow it as fact,
Hooked by his vanity. As for my crew,
I'm sure they'd both endorse my point of view.
I see them now: Chalky, my driver, hard
Middleweight from Bethnal Green, with scarred
Eyebrows, flattened nose, and such a flow
Of hoarse profanity you'd never know
That he was just nineteen and that below
The carapace of toughness you would find
A gentleness surprising as the mind
That in the worst of crises understood
The situation as I rarely could;

He'd grunt his practical advice although
He never let a glimpse of smugness show,
Nor hinted that he thought that he should be
Commander of the tank instead of me.
The gunner, Jim, complete antithesis
Of Chalky but, maybe because of this,
His steadfast mucker, rarely said a word
And, when he did, the tone of voice you heard
Was mild as butter, mellow from the green
Devon hills and fields, the words as clean
As Sunday linen though, when we attacked,
Or were ourselves attacked, he would react
With steely competence and seem to be
A cool extension of the gun that he
With steady concentration aimed and fired.

And now, the man who thinks he holds a key
To wind his soldiers up and then decree
That they be used again in lethal games
Must be dismissed as, in the dark, your names
Chalky and Jim, turn slowly in my mind,
Those unburnt syllables. I hope I'll find
A way to make them breathe. Meanwhile I try
To coax oblivion to where I lie
And roll between my forefinger and thumb
A piece of bread, no bigger than a crumb,
Until it is an amuletic ball
With magic properties that might forestall
Invasion of those images which maul
The unprotected consciousness when sleep
Takes full command and I no longer keep
My regimental mask secure, in place,
And wake at dawn to find my human face
Smeared and wet with tears. *He* must not see
That shameful nakedness exposed, for he
Would claim success for his experiment.
Being as stupid as malevolent
He would not know, nor would he ever know

Those saline exclamation-marks don't show
My mourning, as he understands the word –
No impulse to avenge will have occurred –
Just speechless sorrow as the grit of guilt
That can't, however many tears are spilt,
Be washed away. I shall not fight again.
There are no accusations from the slain,
Nor will there ever be; yet, when that's said,
The spirits or the shadows of the dead
Must be petitioned and appeased. I pray
Into the unresponsive dark that they,
My better, braver, comrades will forgive
Not just this unheroic urge to live
(Small doubt of that) but chiefly this regret
That I must bear the burden and the boon
Of living on beyond their brief forenoon.
I think that they would wish me to rejoice
Without regret and would approve my choice
Of opting for old age in civvy street.
I hope that's so.
                              I don't suppose we'll meet
In some celestial boozer later on,
But one thing is for sure: when I have gone
From this infernal place I may well find
Myself not drinking at, but stuck behind,
Bars of the uncongenial, penal kind.
But I'll get out and then I'll drink to you
Chalky and Jim – and this I hope is true:
As long as I am able to survive,
While I still breathe, I'll keep you two alive.

El Alamein: 50th Anniversary, October 1992

Fifty years! He's old and out of sorts
But still he smiles to see them on the screen,
The lads they were, tin hats, enormous shorts
As big as bivouacs. Full magazine,
One up the spout, going in at the high-port
Through smoke, a newsreel shot in black and white;
A fake for civvies, so he'd always thought;
It wasn't cameras shooting that first night.

And then live interviews – well, just about –
Old men, false teeth and medals, pretty toys
Dangling from their ribbons. Gaunt or stout
They wheeze or croak. Fade out. He hears the noise
Of bugle's rhetoric; then words: *Lest we forget.*
He snorts; then wonders why his face is wet.

A Cemetery Revisited

He has been here before, to this old church
And freshly barbered garden of the dead.
It's almost fifty years since he dug in
And crouched among the consecrated mounds
Marked by stones, not these white lozenges
Paraded here in strict geometries
But ancient, poxed and mossy sepulchres.
At night the mortars and machine-gun fire
Could not quite still the rattling of the cold
White branches of the old ones buried there.

He was one of a small company, though each
Man knew he was alone and wore the same
Coarse battledress of prickly fear and each
Released from queasy heart and lips the same
And nursery prayer which like a tiny rocket
Tried to climb the lacerated sky
Towards a deity who might not yet
Be stunned and deafened by the din below
Of eighty-eights and Nebelwerfers' howls,
Or worse, not deaf, but grown indifferent.

And so he has returned, an old man now.
In autumn's elegiac sunlight he patrols
The files of white stone tablets reading names
And regiments; a few bear pious verses;
Some are nameless, each of these inscribed
Known only unto God. Well, yes, perhaps
Those jigsaw bits of bone and ragged flesh
Have all reassembled in God's head,
A kind of *carnis resurrectionem*.
He turns away, then sees the woman there.

She stands quite still among the rows of graves.
Unnoticed he draws closer, then he sees,
Surprised, her face though turned away from him
Is young, a girl's soft cheek. His heart is tripped
By tender shock to see the wash of tears.
She is too young for mourning yet she weeps,
Perhaps for all the pain and waste of war.
He turns and walks away, does not look back
But knows she'll stay there, patient and alone,
Her tears like scattered seeds on obdurate stone.

On Lover's Walk: 1939

A warm and moon-splashed night on Lovers' Walk,
One war ended, the other not begun;
No noise at closing-time from Belial's boys
Clattering on the cobbles of the Square
South of the border down Mexico way,
Or anywhere; no spies to know that he
Is trembling as she murmurs, moans and moves
Compliant to his touch, mouth opening
Beneath his own; he tastes faint apple-scent
That mingles with a something from the sea
And with a sweetness, too, that hints a rhyme
For lilac trembling in the webby air;
And then his blind and breathless hand is led
To where it meets the source of that small flood,
A melted moon-beam long since drowned and dredged
Emulsive from a deep Sargasso bed,
And he and she are gathered up and flung
Spinning where the constellations wheel.
Dumb thunders shake the skies until the spell
Is spent and they descend to earth and feel
The stillness settle round them like a shawl.
Next morning as he walks to work he sees
The sky squeegeed, unblemished, limpid blue,
A palimpsest of possibility.
On Lovers' Walk the lilac trembles still
And there among the dewy clusters hangs
In naked light a pale and slippery thing,
A slug-like creature at first glance, then seen
For what it is: a grey, translucent bag,
Not large, poetic or American,
Though probably containing multitudes.

Refugees

In dusk of helmet-brims the eyes look stern,
Unwavering; no matter what they see
Or where they gaze – Bluff Cove, Thermopylae,
Kuwait, the Somme – the pillaged cities burn,
And when the owners of those eyes return
And put away their weapons there will be
An alien music in a harsher key,
New words and syntax difficult to learn.

Wars never end. Across the livid plain
The dark processions trail, the refugees,
Anonymous beneath indifferent skies,
Somnambulistic, patient shapes of pain,
Long commentary on war, an ancient frieze
Of figures we refuse to recognise.

The Searchers

We see them on the television-screen,
Each shrunk by distance to a manikin,
Lined up across the moor. They seem to lean
Against the raking wind as they begin
Their slow advance; at every pace they pause
And plunge into the earth before their toes
Their sharpened sticks; then each of them withdraws
His pointed probe and lifts it to his nose.
We know that they are sniffing for a trace
Of carrion from the scabbard of the ground,
And somewhere in that God-forsaken place
The murdered children lie and must be found.

Not on the screen but being watched by it
The man and woman move about the room,
Lift ornaments and put them down, then sit,
Though only briefly, in the curtained gloom,
Until they rise again and climb the stairs
And prowl around the house. They do not speak
And neither sees the pain the other bears,
Nor understands that what they both now seek,
In dazed, somnambulistic wandering
From room to room, will never be revealed:
Forgiveness, that intolerable thing,
Which all their guilt and suffering will not yield.

Old Man in Love

Cocktail of music and wonder dizzies the heart;
Rustle of waters behind the bridal foam,
Voicing various choices never known
Beyond the boundaries of dream or art
Unreels a sonic filament of gold
On which the glittering syllables are hung:
'Oh my dear,' he breathes, 'this love is young,
Although the vessel that it brims is old!'

And, septuagenarian, he capers, sings,
And all that he can carol, call or cry
Is love, the rapturous young love that brings
Him here, to this vertiginously high
Peak of joy where, arms flung wide like wings,
Drunk with his luck, he swears that he could fly.

A Love Song

I've always been in love with you I swear.
'Impossible,' they say, yet it is true:
I speak with certainty, for I was there.

When I reeled groggy as the punchbowl air
Was spiced with melody I longed for you;
I've always been in love with you I swear.

My infant whispers to the beat-up bear
Were meant for you, the tears and kisses too;
I speak with certainty, for I was there.

Let experts, calendars and maps declare
I'm nuts or have at least one wobbly screw;
I've always been in love with you I swear.

New kinds of beauty and the wish to share
These riches were rehearsals, as I knew;
I speak with certainty, for I was there.

Those shadow-loves were work-outs to prepare
For this, the main event, that they led to:
I've always been in love with you I swear;
I speak with certainty, for I was there.

Calculations

All those delicious dancers, the women,
Dreamed temptresses, the shadows on screens;
Sepia-toned goddesses with bald pudenda,
Each breast, like a porcelain-coated half-lemon,
Dappled by foliage in hot magazines,
Even now their memory is able to send a
Shadowy shiver from my early teens.

Also, from novels and poems, I listed
More feminine qualities I could applaud,
And hoped to discover them parcelled in real
Huggable flesh. And so I insisted
No one, except an amalgam of Maud,
Beatrice and Keats' Isabella could steal
My heart from its moorings and tempt it abroad.

When you ask me today, if I find, when I tot
Up the various assets embodied in you,
Every perfection, heroic and lyrical,
How nice to say yes; but it wouldn't be true;
You'd fail as my nonpareil by a long shot,
If the heart's calculations were mathematical
Which, luckily, darling, we both know they're not.

Daily Mail

Morning. Almost nine o'clock. I hear
The metal snap of letter-box, the flop
And skitter on the mat behind the door
        And feel at once the small
Match-like flickering of hope and fear,
Minute, yet still with power enough to stop
The heartbeat for a wink of time before
        I go into the hall.

The usual stuff: I see that I've again
Been chosen to enjoy a holiday
In Tenerife, the latest Ford Gazelle,
        Or fifteen grand in cash;
I'm asked to take my pick, but I refrain.
Nor am I tempted by a fortnight's stay
In Cairo's most luxurious hotel.
        I riffle through the trash:

Invest in Humbro with no risk at all,
Reminders, bills, appeals for *Bosnia Aid*,
CD Classic Club, *The Best of Swing*,
        A postcard from Peru
Signed warmly by a name I can't recall.
A quick re-check as hope begins to fade,
Will die, unless the second post should bring
        That word of love from you.

Bathtimes

I

A strange bath in a small hotel in Durham,
Old fashioned, long, like a porcelain coffin,
He lolls in it and lingers,
Watches, with detachment, pubic hair,
Sparse kelp, thin scrawl on water.
He tries to recollect its dark abundance
When he was young and muscular, but fails,
Or, rather, he recalls it in the head alone
As one remembers dates or names of people
Which freeze, discarnate, in the mind.
He lets his gaze
Drift down to where his toes are visible,
Breaking the steaming surface, and observes
How long his toenails are. They seem to grow
More quickly now as they, he understands,
Will go on growing after he is dead.
The treacherous little bastards are rehearsing.
He nods and smiles a faint sour smile,
And they grin back at him quite equably,
Without the faintest smidgin of remorse.

II

Another bathroom, familiar, his own:
Arctic white of basin, bowl and tub
Is gentled by a fragrant mist;
Silver taps and towel-rail gleam and sweat.
Small waves lap over him.
Promontories of knees protrude like knolls,
The rest of him lagooned, a coral reef.
He stays until the water cools,
Then heaves himself erect,
Reaches for towel and steps on to the mat.
As he begins to dry himself he's pierced
By tiny shock, quick as a single pulse-beat,
The knowledge of another presence there,
And from the corner of his heart he sees,
Behind the film of moisture curtaining
The full-length mirror, movement, form,
A naked woman lifting both her hands
To touch her hair, that lovely gesture like
A Roman amphora made of glowing flesh.
With one swift sweep of towel he wipes the glass
To face a bare and gaunt old man who stares
With still astonished, briefly youthful eyes.

Near the Cliff's Edge

Near the cliff's edge, high above
The restless, dark, white-stippled sea,
A man and woman walk as one;
Their languid steps rhyme perfectly.

The sun is loverlike, is fierce
And yet caressing, jealous too,
Will not permit a single white
Intruder to disturb the blue.

Gorse sweetens the warm soft breeze.
The man and woman pause to kiss
And then move on. Suddenly
He feels disquiet he can't dismiss,

A chilling breath, a faceless fear,
And in this English sun can't guess
Why, amid green abundance, he
Should glimpse a white, blind wilderness,

Great plains of snow and ice, recall
That somewhere he has read or heard
Of two doomed travellers who sensed
The presence of a nameless third.

Love Poet

Of all the poets of his generation
He best explored love's ecstasy and pain,
And overheard the wordless conversation
Of gaze with gaze, and made its meaning plain.

In glinting lyrics, delicate and witty,
He linked the syllables and made a chain
Of images of longing, rage and pity
That shimmered in each reader's heart and brain.

His tolerance and reconciliation
Of opposite emotions seemed divine;
Imagine, then, the general consternation

When he fell sick, grew pale, began to pine,
And failed to diagnose his own condition:
On love he never wrote another line.

Love Lasting

'Love never has lasted for ever,'
       The grey philosopher said,
'Whatever your senses might promise
       Or the poems and novels you've read.

'Like those delectable goodies
       We sucked on when we were young,
Though it lasts a little bit longer,
       It melts quickly away on the tongue.

'And though a faint hint of the flavour
       May linger awhile, when you bite
On another rich chocolate or toffee,
       It's dismissed by this fresher delight.'

'He is wrong,' said the poet to lover,
       'Ignore all that cynical rot;
I know that love *does* last for ever.
       It is lovers alas, who do not.'

Easter Visit

I slipped out of the laundered day and left it there,
Hanging outside the great glass doors to air,
Walked down long corridors that smelt of meals
Or ghosts of meals, past stillnesses on wheels.
I carried gifts of chocolates and fruit,
A yellow fanfare bright against dark suit,
Flowers of resurrection time. I stepped
Dainty through the ward, as one adept
In crossing mined terrain, and reached his bed,
Presented tributary gifts and said
A few rehearsed banalities, sat down
And grinned and nodded like a puppet clown.
I sniffed the scent of darkness in the white
Hygienic lie of air, felt flesh grow tight
On facial bone and scalp until taut skin
Made a *memento mori* of my grin.

I touched his hand and said I had to go.
I think I saw the faintest smile, although
I couldn't swear to that. 'Back soon,' I said,
And moved away with fake reluctant tread,
Then stepped up pace beyond the ward. Outside,
The air was merciless and sweet, denied
Its lightless opposite, and I breathed deep.
Against the sky the building, with a sweep
Of rough-spun shadow, darkened where I stood.
I crossed into the sun, walked fast, felt good.

Wedding Picture

He stands, arranged around his grin
Which, like his posture, seems to be
      Stiff, as if with fear;
Yet something in the lift of chin
And glint of eye suggests that he
      Is happy to be here.

It hints, too, that he thinks he's made
A fine discerning choice in this
      Slight figure at his side,
Whose timid smile might just persuade
Unworldly aunts the altar kiss
      Was all she'd ever tried.

Not so, of course, nor is it true
That he has chosen her from flocks
      Of eager candidates;
There was no breathless female queue
Of aspirants to darn his socks
      Thumping at his gates.

Like all of us, except perhaps
The very beautiful or rich,
      He takes what he can get
('Us' means girls as well as chaps)
And then proceeds to weave and stitch
      A kind of safety-net

Comprising, if not downright lies,
Elaborate hyperbole
      And sonorous pretence,
Which, with luck, might alchemise
To something much like poetry
      And make heart-piercing sense.

Birthday Counsel

for Martin Bax, August 1993

At sixty you are old enough to choose
which path to tread and I believe you can –
Make a choice I mean – take or refuse
What's offered to the not so youthful man.
So out of bed, put on your birthday shoes,
But weigh the odds; don't move without a plan.

Well, that's one policy, the prudent way:
Go cautious to a preselected stage,
Then on towards the next without delay;
Keep clear of bars and you'll escape a cage.
Eat wholesome food, take exercise each day;
Work hard and save three-quarters of your pay.

It seems a doleful prospect, I concede,
But comfort and security must cost
The price of self-denial, though indeed
What you now renounce might well be better lost.
Yet nothing can be firmly guaranteed.
However smart, you could be double-crossed.

Avoid the middle way, the worst of each.
You could try this: dive deep, though not in water;
Choose bodies, booze, and bite the sensual peach,
Savour its squirting juices, yield no quarter
In pleasure's wars; ignore the cant they preach.
This is the sweeter route, though shorter, shorter.

Climacterics

All human lives, except for those which come
With brutal prematureness to a stop
In battle, bedroom, cot or fetid slum
From virus, shrapnel or the gallows-drop,
Ordinary lives, like yours or mine,
Are seen to be, at least in retrospect –
Although they show few traces of design
Imposed by supernatural intellect –
Punctuated by climacterics
Of roughly similar contour, tint and taste.
Those spaced events, the various kicks and pricks,
Chances spurned or fatally embraced,
Moments of supreme, unhoped-for bliss,
Brief and brilliant as a rocket-burst,
Banal and haunting as a covert kiss,
Mined territory triumphantly traversed,
Or negatives of these – a frozen night
Of agony, spiked terror or despair,
Or waking to worse horror in the bright
And pitiless reveille's hostile glare –
We store in mental archives and refer
To those unfaded images when we
Long to know that change can still occur.
No matter what our present state may be,
Even in old age, hope titillates;
Change is possible and might amaze;
At least one more climacteric awaits,
The last perhaps, or so sad reason says.

Lies and Questions

There are some questions nobody should ask,
Though there is always someone to inquire,
'Is that your face or do you wear a mask?'

Whatever you reply they call you liar,
Perhaps with justice. Who for sure can tell?
Better to smile and silently retire.

The anchorite and convict share a cell;
At least the word denotes where they reside
And both could be defined by where they dwell.

But never ask what made each one decide
To turn his back on choice as both have done,
Or whether either, under oath, has lied.

And do not ask of me, or anyone,
If I would die to save a loved one pain
Or worse from sickness, torturer or gun.

For who with certainty can ascertain
If he or she would volunteer to die?
Yet it's been done and might be done again.

Though one loud 'No!' would be my firm reply
I wonder, as I say this, 'Do I lie?'

Night Reflection

Wide-angle shot: the train slides through the night,
Linked carriages, bright vertebrae. It snakes
Through fields and woods, spans rivers, roads and lakes,
Climbs hills or pierces them, going out of sight,
Then reappears and worms across the moors.
Now cut to passenger inside the train,
Alone in his compartment as the rain
Splinters on the window while he snores
Softly to the rocking of his head
From side to side, more or less in time
With flanges' iron tune and pounding rhyme.
Then sleep is splattered suddenly by dread
As violent jerk and shudder of the train
Propel him forward. When he fully wakes
Alarm dissolves: he hears the hiss of brakes
And then, more faint, susurrus of the rain.
The passenger shifts sideways, tries to stare
Through dark, smeared glass, sees nothing of what lies
Beyond but finds himself, with brief surprise,
Faced by someone gazing from out there,
With features very like his own, though more
Cadaverous. Those shadow-brimming eyes,
Their melancholy, seem to advertise
Obscure reproach which troubles him before
Another clanking spasm of the train
Distracts and strenuous wheels begin to turn.
He then discovers that he can discern
Some shadowy pattern of the dark terrain,
Vague, moving shapes of hedgerows, pylons, trees
Behind, or floating through, the spectral head
Like random and repeated thoughts which thread
A string of changing images that tease
At first, then weave their soporific spell.
Then sudden rush and rumble swallow all
In tunnel-gulp and slip impenetrable

Black against the glass, so he can't tell
Whether or not the other is still there
Concealed from him, face pressed against the pane,
Or whether swept away by driving rain;
Or could it be that that ambiguous stare
Will be confronted at the journey's end
When at the exit-barrier he will see
It waiting his arrival patiently
To claim him as accomplice, but not friend?

At the Hotel Metropole

A winter night, the city throbs and thrums.
Lights effervesce in air, or lard the streets
And, fuelled by habit, fear or appetite,
The faceless mites slide past in ones and twos.
The great hotel looms high above the park
And sleek and silent limousines arrive,
Glide silkily towards its aureate jaws,
Once there discharging fragrant skin and furs,
Swept glittering inside to leave behind
A wisp of scent, a trinket's tiny echo.

All warmth within, the foyer shimmers, glows;
Discreet servility in uniform
Greets with pious hands and lowered heads
Privilege and beauty, ushers them
Towards the restaurant where welcome waits
Orchestrally in silver, black and white:
The waiters glide glissando, bow above
Pale naked shoulders. Dishes are conveyed
And covers raised with virtuosic flourish.
Rumours of cold hunger stay outside.

Below, in basement gloom, among the pipes
And coiling wires, the building's viscera,
An alien contraption quietly ticks,
Placed there by serious men who never smile.
In time it will explode and leave behind
A brief and smoky shock of hush before
The shouts and screams, the wheeling ululations,
As medics and police press through the crowds
Who stare with curious hope but only see
Revenge's shattered logic at their feet.

Wearing Out the Dog

We discover, growing older,
April mornings are much colder,
Chilled by what once seemed mild breezes;
Also we confront new teasers
We've not had to puzzle over,
Not till now. Take my dog Rover:
He was euphemistically
'Put to sleep' in January,
Very old and sick poor chappie.
Since he went I've felt unhappy,
Missing those long walks together
We enjoyed in every weather.
Maybe I could do no better
Than to buy another setter.
Yet, despite the joy he'd give me,
He'd most probably outlive me.
That's a sobering reflection.
Here's one more for your inspection:
On my lonely walk this morning
I received a cold wet warning
From my ancient wellies telling
Me they'd sprung a leak and spelling
Out the need for their replacement,
Even in the bargain-basement
Costing plenty. See my trouble?
I'm entangled in a double
Quandary: should I decide to
Buy new boots, and if I tried to
Find a dog like my old prancer,
First I'd have to face this answer:
Which of these would wear out faster?
Boots or owner? Dog or master?

Hetta's Tail

is quite long and slender, tapering to a point,
a sleek-haired whip – appropriately, since she,
its owner, is of the whippet family.
The thing can be disposed in various ways,
curled beneath her haunches, snug between
rear legs whose shape, although she sleeps,
rehearse their tensile power in flight.
When she stretches, waking,
out it comes and, as she rises from her bed,
we see it curving from her rear,
an isolate parenthesis.
In motion it is able to command
a simple semiology,
expressing doubt or disappointment
in drooping stasis; or uncertain hope
with tentative vibrations at the tip.
More often, though, it thrashes table-legs
with rhythmic whiplash clouts
in thrilled anticipation or salute.
It is distinctive, unrelated to
the feathery wafters or blunt twitching stumps
of other breeds.
I watch her now, and she looks back at me.
A small thump on the floor. It seems to say,
'Keep things simple. No matter how you view it,
this is my tail, and I am sticking to it.'

Fictions

I: *Fairplay's Fag*

Michael Fairplay is in his study;
he toasts sausages after footer.
Outside, in wintry twilight,
Mr Clough, crow-black and mortar-boarded,
flaps across the quad in cold pursuit
of miscreants like Arnold Hughes,
the cad, who smokes expensive gaspers,
cuts morning chapel,
bribes or bullies swots to do his Latin prose.
Fairplay's fag brings jam tarts from the tuckshop
and is rewarded with a smile.
He would sooner have had a jam tart
or a sausage,
though which he would've chosen
remains pure speculation.
Later, prep and supper over,
he lies awake among striped snoozers in the dorm
and thinks of home, which is as far away
and beautiful as all of this will seem
in years to come
when he will hear again, in memory,
the owl that calls now from the ivied tower,
echoing in the dark:
Yarooh! it cries. *Yarooh! Yarooh!*

II: *Private Dick*

I quit the bar on East Thirty Second.
It is raining now and starting to get dark.
You can smell it on the sidewalk
after the heat of the past few days;
it hisses under tyres; black umbrellas
gleam slick like seals.
Two, maybe three, blocks away
a police-siren starts to howl.
Someone somewhere is getting hurt
or getting dead.
A wet evening in the city;
I carry gun and licence
and pull my dripping hat brim over eyes.
Whatever or whoever waits for me,
lurking in some alley with the trash-cans and the rats,
or smiling on a high stool in another bar,
I'm good and ready. My gun is loaded,
but I'm not. I take it easy on the sauce.
That's the way it goes
and how it always will, I guess,
leastways while I'm on a case
and that is mostly all the time.
Dumb cops foul up and I am needed then
to put things straight before the next
Missing Person, Fraud or Homicide.
I'd lay an even grand right now
my phone is ringing in the dark.

III: *Steelbrand in Mufti*

Otto von Schnitzel, the master criminal,
sips Dom Perignon '79 and adjusts his monocle.
'You may leave me now,' he says to his henchman,
a hunchback possessed of preternatural strength
despite his hideous deformity,
'but do not relax for a moment your vigilance.
The Englishman could still prove troublesome.'
The Englishman is, of course, none other
than Richard Steelbrand, DSO and bar,
in mufti now the show is over
with the Boche well thrashed and brought to heel,
though Steelbrand serves his country still
in special duties for Intelligence.
At this very moment he approaches
the high walls which surround the castle
where von Schnitzel lurks and like a spider
weaves his web of dark malevolence.
Steelbrand scales the wall and moves towards
the tradesmen's entrance at the rear,
gliding through the darkness like a shadow.
Once inside he makes his way towards
the library where von Schnitzel waits and smiles.
The Englishman is brave enough but foolish.
He will fall into the trap.
The hunchback watches from his hiding-place
beneath the stairs. He sees the Englishman approach,
a cautious silhouette. He holds his breath,
prepares to pounce, then leaps upon his prey.
But Steelbrand is not easily dispatched.
He strikes the snarling villain with a well-timed blow
and sends him sprawling. Quickly he whips out
the strong cord from his pocket and with cool
efficiency he binds the hunchback in a trice
at wrists and ankles, leaves him trussed and gagged,
and climbs the stairs with swift athletic stride,
flings wide the library door and once again

is face to face with his old enemy.
Von Schnitzel rises calmly from his chair
and speaks in silky tones: 'Good evening Major Steelbrand,
I was expecting you. Please raise your hands.'
Steelbrand's stare into the Luger's muzzle
is unwavering. He has faced death too frequently
to be alarmed by one more Hunnish threat.
'You win,' he says, and starts to raise his hands
but in one lithe and fluid movement hurls
himself towards von Schnitzel's knees
and brings him crashing down. The German fires.
The bullet, harmless, finds the library wall.
He drops the Luger and the conflict starts.
Despite his gross physique von Schnitzel, too,
possesses massive strength. He struggles free,
regains his feet and aims a vicious kick,
below the belt, of course, which Steelbrand,
also rising, cleverly evades,
'Infernal cad!' the angry Britisher snaps,
'You'll pay for that!' and in a flash
delivers one straight left which squarely lands
upon his adversary's jaw. The German falls.
Steelbrand has the Luger now.
'We have some matters to discuss,' he says.
'Get on your feet, your hands above your head.
The game is up my friend. Your plot *kaput*.'
But he is not aware that, silently,
behind his back, the handle of the door
is slowly turning. The game is still afoot.

IV: *Spy Story, or Loosely Speaking*

A wet night in Old Compton Street;
the clip-joints and the porn-shops smear
the drizzling dark with yellow light,
and no one spares a second glance
for the man of middle age and size
who, limping slightly, moves towards
the newsagents and goes inside.

Felix Saddler waits upstairs
and hears the slurred iambic step
on bare and creaking boards and knows
Charles Loosely has arrived on time.
He pours two single malts and smiles
as Loosely's head peers round the door.
'It's good to see you Charles,' he says.
'Sit down, let's hear the latest score.'

Loosely takes his seat and sips
his malt and nods and then he speaks:
'You won't be too surprised to hear
that "Nimrod" is wrapped up at last.
Once Petrie's cover had been blown
I knew the handwriting and guessed
they'd snared him with a honey-trap,
and I was right. We shut up shop.
Pavement-artists kept an eye
on his old letter-box and drop.
We sent the babysitters home
when everything was clear as day.
I knew the rot was bound to come
once redbrick people were let in.
The talent-spotters must be mad –
next thing, we'll find them focusing
on sixth-form Comprehensive oiks.
We're old hands Felix, you and I,
and know how hush-hush outfits play.

There had to be a mole, of course,
and all the signs led back to base;
each signal, coded or *en clair*,
said just one thing: like chastity
betrayal starts at you-know-where.'

Felix Saddler's face is white
and suddenly his eyes are bright
with knowledge or perhaps with pain.
He says, 'You mean to say the mole...'
and leaves the question hanging there.

Loosely nods just once; his face
shows no expression. 'Yes, the mole
is who it always had to be.'

'Not Angelino or the Pole?'
asks Felix Saddler hopelessly.

A faint smile plays on Loosely's lips:
'I think you know Control's the mole.'

'The mole? Control!'

             'Control's the mole.
Come Felix, we have things to do.
It's time, I think, we took a stroll.'

My New Book

It's scheduled to be published in July.
The bids to serialise are running high
And movie rights were snapped up weeks ago
For what you might describe as mega-dough.
The TV channels scramble in a queue
To book me for a prime-time interview
And all the major bookstores want to fix
Signing sessions here and in the sticks.
Wait till you see the jacket! David's done
A kind of symphony of sea and sun
With subtle hints of sexuality
And darker shades of our mortality.
What's that you said? What is the book about?
You'll have to stick around to find that out,
But not for long. I'll finish it, no sweat.
I've never failed to meet a deadline yet.

Makers and Creatures

It is a curious experience
And one you're bound to know, though probably
In other realms than that of literature,
Though I speak of poems now, assuming
That you are interested, otherwise,
Of course, you wouldn't be reading this;
It is strange to come across a poem
In a magazine or book and fail
At first to see that it's your own.
Sometimes you think, grateful and surprised,
'That's really not too bad', or gloomily:
'Many have done as well and far, far better'.
Or, in despair, 'My God, that's terrible.
What was I thinking of to publish it!'
And then you start to wonder how the great
Poets felt, seeing, surprised, their poems
As strangers, beautiful. And how do all the
Makers feel to see their creatures live?
The carpenter, the architect, the man who
Crochets intricate embroideries
Of steel across the sky. And how does God
Feel, looking at his poems, his creatures?
The swelling inhalation of plump hills,
Plumage of poplars on the pale horizon,
Fishleap flashing in pools cool as silver,
Great horses haunched with glossy muscles,
Birds who spray their song like apple juice,
And the soft shock of snow. He must feel good
Surprised again by these. But what happens
When he takes a look at man? Does he say,
'That's really not too bad', or does he, as I fear,
Wince once and mutter to himself:
'What was I thinking of publishing that one?'

Likenesses

What did He really look like?
None of the gospels says.
The holy shroud of Turin
Is a kind of paraphrase

Of all those long-nosed gloomies
From Byzantium and Rome.
Blake was quite convinced
We should look much closer to home.

'Spindle-nosed rascals,' he called them,
Those images of Our Lord,
Travesties of the features
Of the Messiah he adored.

'Jesus Christ was a snubby,'
Blake asseverated, no doubt
With a sidelong glance in the looking-glass
At his own diminutive snout.

Ice Bucket

'...all the wedding gifts were on display,
and guess what William's Uncle Peter sent –
not something that we'd bring out every day,
but sweet of him, he's such an innocent –
an ice-bucket! Oh no, you silly thing,
not 'nice'! I said the word quite clearly, 'ice'!
Hugh managed somehow not to lose the ring.
I'm glad they threw confetti and not rice
like years ago they did...'
                                    attention strayed
as Annie's avian voice went twittering on
and I reflected on that bucket made
of glittering ice and, after she had gone,
regretted that I'd not discovered more
about this frozen artefact which could
serve as a poetic metaphor
though not, perhaps, one easily understood,
if hardly as a practical device
for drawing water and for washing floors.
It might be fun – though purchased at a price –
to set about some ordinary chores
and fill it with hot water and then see
its slow becoming its own burden till
contents and container all ran free
in one expanding flood of overspill
requiring a prosaic bucket made
of plastic or of metal to convey
the shining thing, once lovely, now betrayed,
outside the kitchen to be sluiced away.

Junk

It was a leisure-day, called 'holiday'
Only by the very few and old
Though none of these could quite remember why
The word had once possessed a gleam of gold
And still awakened distant silver sounds.
The city glittered; citizens patrolled
The areas reserved for exercise.
Among those walking in the public grounds
A young man and his son, a child of eight,
Moved towards that section of the town
Preserved by civic law in just that state
It wore in 1985, a place
For tourists, amateurs of history
And relic-hunters. There, the man and boy
Stood before a window which displayed
Disordered curiosa: garments, toys,
Primitive machines, containers made
From substances of unknown origin,
Crude metal weapons that, in ancient wars,
Were operated manually. A skin
Of extinct animal, that once was worn
For warmth, and also as a mark of caste,
By someone's female forebear, now adorned
A cabinet composed of genuine wood.
But of that dusty salvage from the past
One object seized the boy's attention: shaped
Like an oblong box, its lifted lid
Showed no interior but solid stuff
In slender layers. Its contents were itself.
The puzzled child said to his father, 'Look!
What's that thing over there?'

                    The father's brow
Showed momentary perplexity, then cleared:
'Oh that. I think it's what they called a book.'
'What did they use it for?' the child inquired.
'I'm not quite sure. I think my grandpa told me
Long ago, but I've forgotten now.'

England

a patriotic poem

Some call her Mother, but I feel
More like a husband than a son.
I need her, I suppose, but not
With ardour and she irritates
More often than she pleases me;
And only when I'm flirting with
Some hot exotic charmer do
I start to value her good points,
And then, of course, with itching guilt.
She nags. Just when you're feeling good
And one more drink would do the trick
She says: 'That's all. You know you'll make
An idiot of yourself. You might
Start dancing or reciting poems.'
Then there are moments when she kicks
Her heels and all my previous
Impressions of her character
Moonhigh. But these are rather rare.
Sometimes I've slipped away from her
And lolled with strangers in the sun,
But then I find I'm missing her.
And though she looks so stern in those
Hoarse tweeds and stomping shoes she wears
On most occasions, yet there are
Sudden times and places when
She looks so beautiful you want
To say you'd give your life for her,
Almost sure the words are true.
And yet, well, probably the next
Week or even day you'll find her
Back to normal, dressed in hessian,
Whining like a carpet-sweeper –
You'd hardly credit she can sing!

There's one thing though, she always makes
Certain that you're comfortable,
Sees your underwear is laundered,
Feeds you on a balanced diet.
But there's the snag. It's dull. And yet
You can be sure – however wild –
She'd never stick a knife in you.
We've had our rows like everyone,
Some bitter; but despite my threats
I've never seriously thought
Of getting a divorce. For one
Thing it would cost too much;
Besides, I don't think I could live
For any length of time without
My – yes, there is no other word
But I must whisper it – my love.

Dominoes

i
This is a good game:
Black clatter. Turn one over,
Small, starry midnight.

ii
The gentlest of games:
No complaints of domino
Hooliganism.

iii
Medals are not won.
No one has been known to knock
Spots off anyone.

iv
Old men in corners,
Caps, mufflers, glasses of mild;
Clicking of old bones.

Coup de Grâce

The hurt will carry you beyond all pain.
Duck if you can but, if you move too late,
The big fist zooming in can't strike again.

No matter how religiously you train
To tip the scales at your best fighting-weight
The hurt will carry you beyond all pain.

Just one brief brilliant starburst in the brain,
Then darkness drowns ambition, love and hate;
The big fist zooming in can't strike again.

You always knew one blow would end your reign
So if, tonight, this proves to be your fate,
The hurt will carry you beyond all pain.

This is the way things are: you can't complain
That insult comes with mercy on one plate;
The big fist zooming in can't strike again.

All words of consolation must seem vain,
And yet I see some cause to celebrate:
The hurt will carry you beyond all pain;
The big fist zooming in can't strike again.

Taking a Dive

'Stand up and be counted!' they said.
'Be resolute and strong!'
There was only one of me
So the counting wouldn't take long;
But, all the same, I lacked
As ever both bottle and clout,
So I lay down and was counted
        Out.

Views and
Distances

Unreliable Assumptions

Hand-in-hand, smiling as they stroll,
The elderly man and woman pause to nod
Back at the municipal geraniums
Before resuming their unhurried trail
Towards the café near the swings and slide.

It would be easy to assume that this
Old couple had witnessed the dear, swift flight
Of fifty years or more of matrimony.
Not so. They met a month ago, or less,
At the *Darby and Joan* in Mercury Street.

It is unwise to make assumptions from
Observed appearances and signs. The roar
Of honking laughter from the Red Lion snug
Might mask distress, could even hide the dumb
Misery of absolute despair.

When my old friend, George Carmody, was seen
Leaving All Hallows after matins that Sunday,
And yet again at evensong, one might
Guess that he, improbably, had been
Converted, late, to Christianity.

But no, as Carmody himself confessed,
He had followed down the street a girl in frail
And flowery dress, sweet brevity of which
Revealed the longest, loveliest bare legs
That ever made eyes pop and breathing stall.

Those sleek and beckoning limbs had led him there
To lurk in musty shadows near the font
And watch the holy shaft of sunlight coax
Her hair to fine-spun gold, while bluish air
Was stained with rose-breath, wax, psalms' bready scent.

For most of that long summer Carmody
Was seen on Sunday in the sacred house.
Though there for heathen reasons, might not he
Have found in sermon, hymn and litany
At least a rumour of God's love and peace?

Well, no. Each Sunday, breathing pious air,
He had never felt more hopelessly alone,
And gazing at her aureate head would groan
Beneath the heavy sadness of desire,
Learn nothing that he had not always known.

Billets Aigres

Early autumn, the first week
of October and a new love,
as leaves were turning in the watered milk
of morning mist they heard the click
in the hall and the sound of the fall,
not of sere leaves but the morning mail,
and with it a postcard, the first
of what would become a flood,
each picked for its power to shock, stop breath:
images of terror, torture, death.

At first by serious artists – Dürer,
Bosch and Munch – then came cruder cards,
each more violent and obscene,
and on the backs of all were scrawled
in a spiky hand he recognised
variations on one bleak theme,
short and soundless yelps of rage
and hatred. Every weekday morning
for more than eighteen months one dropped
from the letter-box. And then they stopped.

First they felt tentative relief and doubt;
then the sweet detoxifying silence grew,
and they began almost to forget
those daily shafts of hatred and the threats,
forgetting, too, the woman who
had uttered them, till one evening as he sat,
peaceful with Donne's poems on his lap,
a card fluttered down like a leaf from the sky –
a calm Corot landscape – and on the yellowing back
in that same spiky scrawl: 'I shall love you dear heart till I die'.

The Ghosts of Love

In the calm darkness of the moonless nights
those almost silent whisperings are heard:
the ghosts of love perform their timeless rites.

Not lovers' ghosts but shades of love's delights
return to haunt, with sigh or murmured word,
in the calm darkness of the moonless nights.

A disembodied voice of air recites
its litany of loss and, disinterred,
the ghosts of love perform their timeless rites.

The icy call of owl and star invites
the jilted lover to make up a third
in the calm darkness of the moonless nights.

Each place where passion flowered and rose in flights
of petals will remember this occurred:
the ghosts of love perform their timeless rites.

Though carnal vases may be smashed, their plight
beyond all aid, pathetic or absurd,
in the calm darkness of the moonless nights
the ghosts of love perform their timeless rites.

The Long Honeymoon

They had been warned by the grey sages,
through homily or hint; not only though
by these, but others, too,
through word of mouth or print –
agony aunts and jaundiced divorcees –
that sexual passion could not ever last.

But they ignored all warnings
and advice; they settled down together
to discover, after ten years,
the sweet and heady spice
of carnal love no less delicious, even
tastier than it had been in the past.

Only last night they each
explored the other as if they'd never known
those parts before, writhing
in warm conjunction, rolling over,
recumbent dance, the bed their ballroom floor;
and then they slept, in stillness, like the dead.

Yet dawn saw them awake
to dance again, tempo more andante,
twirls less wild, but never
a touch of weariness or strain.
Next evening, when he whispered, 'Bed?' she smiled.
'I think I'm just a bit too tired,' she said.

Changing Roles

Where are those lovely girls we used to know,
The dreamy Juliets and cool Cordelias,
Vivacious Rosalinds and pale Ophelias,
Tall tigerish Helens, the dark or golden flow
Of all that lustrous, lilac-scented hair
Now all of them have taken different parts?
Where are those smiles that pierced our panting hearts,
The creamy robes of flesh they used to wear?

They've put on wiry wigs and wrinkled masks;
They move arthritically and sing like crows.
I wonder though if any of them asks,
'Whatever happened to those Romeos?'

A few might just be trusted with a spear,
But most look like that mad old fool King Lear.

The Emperor's Daughter

Exquisite and bare
beneath the silken duvet
no lover may share

she smiles, nearing sleep,
and counts her hapless suitors
trailing past, like sheep.

Les Belles Dames

Reflected in the troubled looking-glass
of tall shop-windows' tilted, smooth lagoons,
not plain enough for you to make a guess
at colour of the eyes, or even hair –
except that you would know it dark or fair –
they haunt these late autumnal afternoons.

Their other, more substantial, avatars,
released from vitreous immurement, seem
even less attainable than those,
though no less lovely as their dainty feet
chatter like castanets along the street,
while they dance out of sight and into dream.

Their milieu is the City – Rome, New York,
Paris, the Smoke. They are not Zion's daughters,
with wanton eyes and undulating walk,
whose haunches mime the ocean's heaves and dips
and signal to the punters: *Read my hips* –
their message faintest music over waters.

There is, for thwarted seekers, only this
hope of something like a rendezvous,
which has to be in sleep's metropolis
where, white and slender in blue evening air,
as innocent as cigarettes once were,
they open wide their arms; then fade from view.

Lost Properties

These are not docketed and tidied away
in cabinets on main-line railway stations
but are scattered over tracts of time and place
to be revisited, perhaps, but never
reclaimed. Item: a pair of flimsy yellow
knickers seen on a Sunday morning, tangled
in brambles on the edge of Roundhay golf-course;
and, later on the same day – or so it now seems –
close to the lake in the park, on unstartled
grass, a single red shoe with stiletto heel,
sad in its abandoned, tawdry elegance.

I do not think it likely that there could be
two different owners of these lost properties,
nor am I confident that I shall ever
see their bereft possessor, though a small wick
of hope is not quite extinguished. I return
quite often to these sedgeless, unchanged places,
and, though it may be revenant rather than
corporeal woman haunting the lakeside,
I feel one day she might appear, limping
on single red stiletto heel, the pale curve
of cold cheeks vulnerable in songless air.

Doctors

Doctors walk swiftly down corridors and wear
white coats with stethoscopes dangling either from
their pockets or worn like drab chains of office.
Men and women, they are all young, well under
forty, and all of them are very handsome.
When they smile, mischievous at the pretty nurse
or reassuringly at the aged patient,
it is with teeth perfectly white and even.

These are the doctors we see on our screens
and they do not much resemble the ones we meet
in shabby consulting-rooms whose smiles, if there,
are rather tired and probably display teeth
not quite the white of fresh aspirin as they
enquire about bowel-movement, waterworks
and known allergies to antibiotics
before tapping out nostrums on computers.

Other doctors exist or have existed
of course but these, too, aren't likely to be seen
in TV soaps wearing dangling stethoscopes,
for these are the Teachers, Doctors of Music,
Philosophy, Literature and Law, many
quite famous and revered though not for white smiles
or dark curly hair: Doctors Johnson and Donne
and the composer of *Rule Britannia*, Arne.

There are also Doctors of Divinity
and Doctors of the Church, Aquinas, Anselm,
Teresa of Avila, Francis of Sales,
to be revered though not carnally desired.
But when molested by pains and lack of breath
it is the unglamorous, overworked man
or woman we seek out, not the beautiful
or the holy who would frighten us to death.

Rough Boys

was a common appellation in my childhood
for describing lads from families and districts
even poorer than our own. 'Rough' was relative
of course. To the elegant and perfumed mothers
of the blazered and well-shod boys from the houses
with gardens, whose dads worked in banks or offices,
my brother Ken and I would have been considered
unquestionably rough. No doubt Mrs Spender
would have been careful to keep little Stephen
safe from the risk of meeting one or both of us.

But there were rougher boys, by far, than Ken and me.
I'll name a few: Stink Holbrow, Doggie Percival,
Dump Rickard, Mockle Welch and Chinaman Cheney,
all of them addressed, as you see, by soubriquets.
We did not know their Christian names, each cognomen
as mysterious then as now, except for Stink,
whose pungent presence could have been detected in
blindfold darkness at a dozen paces or more.

Chinaman Cheney was killed at Narvik. Rickard
died early from strong drink, or so it was rumoured.
As for the others, I have lost all trace of them
but, whether living or dead, they have become ghosts,
still scowling their menace from corners in ginnels
or swearing and spitting on the truant towpath
of the Grand Union Canal, where they still wait
to ambush their victims, sissies with neat partings
and leather satchels holding virtuous homework,
the rough boys who don't grow old as we who are left
with our given names grow old or invisible;
and when, in the whispering classroom, the register
is called, all, present or absent, answer their names.

The K.O. Culture

Differences were settled with a punch,
Though crack of fist on jaw would always seem
Too sharp, the sound of speeding billiard-balls
Colliding with abrupt and bony *clack*;
No real punch on the jaw could sound like that.
But these encounters happened on the screen,
And we believed, in some platonic sense,
That those right-hooks were real, not like our own
Wild swings in back street, bar or football-stand,
Which missed completely or smashed up your hand,
And hurt the striker far more than the struck.

Our heroes and exemplars might be tough
Stetsoned cowpokes wearing neckerchiefs,
Leathery chaps in leather chaps and spurs,
Whose fist-fights were conducted in the bars
Of honky-tonk saloons; or they could be
Gangsters in fedoras, just as quick
With uppercut or haymaker as gun.
But these were not the only ones who punched;
Even Catholic priests could use their mitts.
You hardly ever saw a film in which
No character got walloped on the chin.

Even debonair society dudes,
When cross, or crossed in love, knocked culprits cold.
Remember them? Tuxedoed, brilliantined,
The Roberts – Taylor, Young, Montgomery –
William Powell and Melvyn Douglas, all
Capable of flattening a cad
As coolly as they lit a cigarette
In frothy comedies. It's what they did,
And what we did as well, or not so well,
Or tried our best to do if we were mocked,
Insulted, wronged in any way. We socked.

And, as I've said, we often missed or bust
Our fist on ivory skull, or else we found
Ourselves entangled with the adversary,
Undignified and rolling on the ground.
Absurd. And yet one sometimes heaves a sigh
For those, the K.O. days, when we replied
To insult with a quick right-cross. Or tried.
Surely better than the baseball-bat,
Machete, knife or, worst of all, the gun
That now replace the fist, off-screen and on –
If things have ever truly been like that.

In Regent's Park

Above the tower-blocks' squinting geometries
A homing jet slides down the silky sky,
Its human freight invisible to us
As we to them with those things we can see,
Slow juggling of bright traffic lights, the heap
Of crumpled misery slumped upon the bench
Inside the park, whose mimicry of sleep
Permits no rest or respite from the stench
Of what he has become. No healing dreams
For him and yet, close by, in that same park,
The famous summer Dream unfolds and holds
Both players and an audience that seems
Entranced, although two folk from Portland, Maine,
Express vague puzzlement because, for them,
Ass and Bottom are straight synonyms.

Delivering the Goods

1: Good in Bed

An expression used more in literary
dialogue, perhaps, than in quotidian
exchanges among friends and acquaintances;
a term that is employed far more frequently
by women (both fictive and real) than by men,
usually referring to the other sex.
This, if true, may be because of the greater
spiritual generosity of women
who are more often ready to discover
some small saving virtue in the otherwise
entirely contemptible male.
                              We all know
what is meant of course, in a general way,
yet nevertheless this conjunction of words
transmits semantic discords: for example,
is the man or woman who is 'good in bed'
good only in bed? Does virtue leak away
when a vertical position is assumed?
Surely such moral exemplars as Mother
Teresa were as good in bed as they were
out of it.
                  Origen must have been as good
as it is possible to be, according
to his own beliefs, for Eusebius claimed
that this wise and virtuous philosopher
removed from his own body those instruments
which occasion sin; or, to put it plainer,
he cut his bollocks off.

                                                                      But of course we know
that the 'good' in 'good in bed' does not imply
moral rectitude, but this is not to say
its opposite is necessarily there.
The 'good in bed' must be imaginative,
inventive, tender, grateful and unselfish,
qualities that even Origen would not
condemn when exercised in other places.
But, however passionate the players seem,
they will not be truly good unless each knows,
after the fierce fortissimo crescendo,
the sigh, in the dark, of love's unfolding rose.

II: *Good for Nothing*

Good for nothing, a favourite phrase
My father used as he would glower,
Enraged by what I seemed to him to be;
Of course I knew, by his fierce gaze
And look of chewing something sour,
He did not mean to praise or flatter me.

The words themselves, though, puzzled me
Whichever way I looked at them,
For *good* and *nothing* didn't seem to mate,
Would always, surely, disagree
Like *precious fake* or *worthless gem*;
I couldn't see what they might designate.

Good was fine and positive
While *nothing* was – well, vacancy;
And I – the Old Man claimed – was good for this;
How I, or anyone, could give
Virtue to sheer nullity
Was quite beyond me then, and it still is.

He called my brother, Kenneth, *ape*
And rarely used his given name.
I was a *pup*. I think perhaps his head
Held beasts, whose one way of escape
Was through his mouth. Was he to blame?
Who knows, or cares, now that the bastard's dead?

III: *Good Eggs*

From the fridge he carefully selects
two eggs and holds them both in the palm
of his left hand for her inspection.

They are smooth and brown. She nods assent,
then takes them from him and, with a pin,
deftly pricks the rounder end of each.

Next, she places both eggs in a bowl
of warm water, second stratagem
against their cracking. Her final trick

is to add a generous pinch of salt
to the bubbling water in the pan.
Then it is for him to take the eggs,

one at a time, in a table-spoon,
from the warm bowl and transfer them to
the boiling water. He checks the clock,

then watches as she lays out the plates,
spoons and cups while the eggs are nudging
each other in the steaming saucepan.

It is good again to watch her move
about the room, graceful though without
self-consciousness, and he is surprised

by a sudden pinprick of bright joy
that these shared simplicities should bring
a new-laid world, fresh every morning.

IV: *Good Grief*

It is not here among the fragrant rites,
The flowers and summer dresses in the cool
Twilight of the nave where slanting lights
From clerestory and gilded oriel fall,
Gleaming softly on the polished box
Which, to our puzzled eyes, seems far too small
To hold his broken body and which mocks
Our shattered notions of the brave and tall;
Nor can the muted music's wiliest arts –
His favourite Dvořák, Beethoven and Brahms –
Coax it to the chill vault of our hearts
Or hold us safe in reassuring arms.

Though those diminished sevenths seem to float
The scent of all June's flowers made audible,
And loop a noose of honey round the throat,
We find their blandishments implausible.
Some facile tears expressed, a sob or two,
But grief, true grief, is scentless, drab, elsewhere,
And that elsewhere, which waits for me and you
Beyond the cypress, marble crosses, square
White or lichened tablets of carved stone,
Is silent, cold, and it will not permit
Entry save to those who are alone;
And this is where we must contend with it,
The grief that does not heal or mitigate
The pain of loss, yet must be understood
As necessary and will predicate
Its cauterizing hurt as final good.

V: *Good at English*

He never was much good at school,
Couldn't bowl and couldn't bat;
On the football field a fool,
And in the classroom worse than that,
        Except, of course, at English.

Mathematics baffled him;
He had no memory for dates;
Latin made his poor head swim
But he could quote you scads of Yeats,
        For he was good at English.

Almost bottom of the form,
Main butt of masters' dusty wit
And bait for bullies in the dorm,
It did not seem to help a bit
        That he was good at English.

Nor did it help when, schooling done,
He sought employment which might bring
Wealth and status, even fun,
But found there was no opening
        For someone good at English.

At last he got a job and still
Works there, at the G.P.O.,
Selling stamps behind a grille
To people who will never know
        That he was good at English.

At home he keeps a family –
A wife who fades, two boys who grow –
And he and they would all agree
He's not much good at that, although
        He once was good at English.

VI: *Good Citizen*

At the edge of the copse, nervous branches
squirm before his face.
He watches, does not move close.
The child's gold head pores over buttercups,
parasoling daisies. She is very beautiful.
The mother smiles dreamily in the sun.
When both have gone he shrugs the shadows off
and walks towards the town.

Next morning he catches his usual train.
Opposite are biteable thighs, smooth knees
like new potatoes. He raises his paper and reads
black commentaries. The air
quivers with lavender and musk.
The carriage sways and stumbles on the rails,
strains against thrust. He lowers his paper
and stares her boldly in the knees.

On Sunday morning the cat on his lawn
holds a bird in its mouth; the seeds of its eyes
are alive and bright. The cat is proud.
He eats roast lamb for lunch, then sleeps.
On his way to evensong he bows
to familiar faces on the street.
He is the good citizen, the friendly neighbour.

VII: *Good Time*

How that ravenous abstraction, Time,
can own the quality of goodness, goodness
knows; and yet we say it all the time.

Have a good time is simple, I suppose;
at least we catch the drift: enjoy yourself,
get drunk, get laid, get tanned, or all of those.

Joy buds and flowers in Time, that's understood;
that which is indispensable to bliss,
its soil and habitation, must be good.

But when they say, as they quite often do,
all in good time, what can be meant by this?
I've used the phrase myself, and so have you.

No one, though, has ever told us why
the time is 'good' that everything is in:
I can't explain, however hard I try.

Language games are always hit or miss;
you might not learn much but they can be fun.
In fact I had a good time writing this.

Hearing Aid

'Leopards pray,'
the surpliced voice intoned
from the Sunday morning radio.

The listener saw the furry creatures,
paws together, eyes half-closed,
a scene that William Blake might have composed.

On *The World at One*
a different voice spoke of the need
for screaming pregnant women,

and the same listener saw
shrill images from Bosch or Fuseli
of female suffering and man's indifference.

Later in the day, on Radio 4,
a play was trailed: *Goats*, by Henry Gibson;
a bucolic comedy, no doubt.

And then the listener's wife
said, 'I've found it. Here. You left it in the loo,
as you so often do.'

Evening: Radio 3.
The Great C Major, words now clear,
the image vivid, too:

Tall, muscular and lean
in full dress uniform,
a stern, bemedalled Royal Marine.

Yorkshire Dandy

On Friday night you might observe him,
    a man of uncertain years
dressed in reactionary clothing
    who nevertheless appears
to display a certain stylish elegance
    that you do not often see
at any time in the centre of
    Otley and most certainly
not at 10pm in Boroughgate
    where already evidence
of an over-indulged appetite
    for a superabundance
of Tetley's bitter and fish and chips
    may be detected upon
the pavement where he carefully steps
    as he, too, is eating from –
not polystyrene or *The Bradford*
    Telegraph and Argus – but
The Times Literary Supplement
    and his hot supper is not
fishcake, cod, haddock, or even plaice,
    but sole meunière with what
else but *frites* and his belly contains
    a chilled Chardonnay and not
ten pints of Tetley's or John Smith's,
    nor does he bellow randy
needs to deaf skies or, alfresco, piss
    for he is the Yorkshire Dandy.

Al Bowlly on the Costa Del Sol

Afternoon in February.
Back in England poor sods shiver,
or so we meanly hope.
Here, in Andalucia, tingling sunshine
ices walls and terraces
and turns the iron grills
to fancy liquorice sticks.
We sit in our white room, the window wide,
eating bread and olives,
drinking *vino tinto*
while the radio plays
songs from those camphor-scented days
between the two Great Wars.

The tempo sets
bunioned feet tap-tapping to the beat
and, somewhere else,
yet also somehow here,
the dancers take the floor.
The men's strong arms
lightly hold the sweet and lovely girls
with something in their eyes,
not quite angelic now
that angels are so few
but, while at least the songs are sung,
they'll string along with you.

So close your eyes
and rest your head
here on my shoulder while,
in the haunted ballroom, tall
and handsome dancers in white ties and tails
take partners for the last waltz and begin
their graceful circumambulations till
the saxophones have melted to a slur
of liquid silver on the midnight floor
and all the dancers turn and turn,
like those old HMVs
which, once they'd sung their song,
slowed down and down and then, at last, were still.

Drink Problem

You should not trust the testimony of drunks.
They romanticise what is, at best,
a risky pleasure and, at worst,
a dark seductress who will kill when minded to.
But look – I, too, have started on the game
of making metaphors, mythologising
in the usual woolly way
of shabby poets with red eyes and noses
and hands that shake. It will not do. Dismiss
those tales of noble topers, the eloquent and wild,
bardic boozers, holy fools, the brilliant and the doomed.
Recognise the drab or foul realities:
vomit, shame, remorse, the fractured mind
and furred intelligence, the taste of knives,
and, always there, the metaphysical stink
that drenches you and can't be washed away.
This is the drunkard's lot; the briefest glance –
like this one now,
side-long, shifty, quick to slither off –
is quite enough to drive a wagon-load
of sober prosemen straight on to the booze.

Negative Reflections on Aquinas

I have managed to resist, without too much distress,
The temptation to read *Summa Contra Gentiles*,
And my favourite bedside reading has never been
Summa Theologica. I recall having seen,
Or heard, that Saint Thomas Aquinas somewhere claims
That the Saved in Heaven can look down at the flames
Of Hell through a handy peep-hole in Paradise,
Savouring the torments of the Damned by this device.

Proclaimed Doctor of the Church in 1567,
Aquinas promised that we could get to Heaven
If we followed this piece of advice: 'Live each day
As if it were your last.' There must be another way.

Your last? Live every single day of your life in stark
And gibbering terror of the coming dark? No way.

Close Shave

Morning clangs outside in North Street, Otley.
On with – once again – the shabby motley.
Before that, though, a piss and then a shave;
And so it goes, and will go, to the grave.

You start the tedious ritual once more
And smear your chops, as you have done before
A thousand times, with Father Christmas stuff;
And then you scrape away the feathery fluff.

One little nick. Not bad. It's time to rinse
And dry your face, splash aftershave and wince
At styptic on the cut. The sting soon goes;
Ahead, the day's grey page of turbid prose.

How many more small cuts and shaves remain?
You'd rather not be told. But this is plain:
That's one less scrape-and-lather to be done.
And is this any consolation? None.

Another View of Thanatos

Death be not proud! Why not? You've got good cause.
Mighty and dreadful? Yes, we're bound to call
You both of these since you have fathered all
Our best achievements, art and healing, laws,
Rituals to ease the pain that gnaws
On hearts and minds till desperations scrawl
Their shrill graffiti on the falling wall:
You justly claim respect, if not applause

But few of us will tender thanks though you
Persuade us to erect great domes of thought
And palisades of piety to thwart
Your fruitful menaces. Yet this is true:
You frighten me to death old sport;
If I had half your power, then I'd swank too.

In the Chair

Steel bangles clamp wrists;
head is half-nelsoned by a rigid arm,
feet fastened firm.

Buttocks are clenched like fists;
I am not comfortable
but do not complain.

I would be content to sit here
for a very long time,
forever if I could.

But I know, almost,
that in seconds I must go.
The bald walls blur,

voices in the gallery
melt to a running slur.
Soon I shall be a nasty memory.

Blind, between my thighs,
my sex is shrivelled to a dead wince,
could cause now little offence

as out of sight, anonymous,
the clean hand reaches for the switch
to grasp and throw it down.

I will sit this dance out
as the lights in the cell-blocks dim
and the orchestra of mugs and spoons begins.

Aubade

'Rain before dawn,'
is what the weather-forecaster had said,
and he was right.
I heard it niggling at the window-pane
when I awoke,
uneasy in the deep, unsleeping night.

It was also
sweeping, with soft and patient industry,
pavements and roads,
gleaming feebly in the dark below.
The world might be
a little cleaner when the sun arose.

When the first, faint
intimation of almost light slid
a slender strip
of steeliness between thin curtain-gap
I heard a sound
quite different from the rainfall's hiss and tap.

It was the drum
of marching feet approaching close, and then
abrupt full-stop
of studs. A yelped command to load, then slam
of rifle-bolts.
It could have been a dream, but it was not.

Overheard in the Students' Bar

'Hi! What you got in that blue file?'

'My essay for old Zimmermann.
I should a finished it last week
but I kept stalling. Then I ran
clean out of all excuses, so
stayed up all night to finish it.
That's why I'm feeling knackered now.'

'Yeah, I thought you looked like shit.
What's your essay all about?'

'Hopkins's Terrible Sonnets.'

'Who
was Hopkins then?'

'Oh, some old priest,
a Jesuit.'

'And was it true?'

'What true?'

'His sonnets, were they all
really terrible? If so
how come he got to publish them?'

'Yeah, pretty awful. I don't know.'

Small Expectations

The promised pleasure comes at last, then goes
So swiftly, leaving little after-taste.
Is this the most we can expect? God knows.

In summer's drought we long for winter snows.
They fall and melt away to leave bleak waste;
The promised pleasure comes at last, then goes.

The steely river melts and water flows.
Spring's brief refurbishment is soon defaced.
Is this the most we can expect? God knows.

At last the ardent lover holds the rose
Of long desire, that creaminess unlaced.
The promised pleasure comes at last, then goes.

And is there nothing more she can disclose?
Must every gem reveal itself as paste?
Is this the most we can expect? God knows.

Not all caresses surely, turn to blows,
Nor every dainty maiden prove unchaste?
The promised pleasure comes at last, then goes.
Is this the most we can expect? God knows.

Barometers of Fashion

When Uncle Walter died he left behind
A heap of clothes, all of them consigned
To me, drab legacy. Walter had been
A man of substance, physically I mean,
Well over six feet tall and hefty, too.
So, of those suits and jackets, very few
If any would be worn by me, although
Among the camphor-scented pile I spied
One garment that I just might wear outside
The privacy of home. I pulled it out,
An overcoat of heavy stuff, about
Half a century old, but still quite smart,
Expensive triumph of the cutter's art.

This was the winter of 1963
And though the coat was far too big for me
The vicious icy weather swept away
What doubts I might have felt. So I went swathed
From chin to ankles, hem an inch or so
Above the ground and trailing in the snow.

The first time that it went on public show
Was in 'The George' saloon, Great Portland Street
Where BBC producers used to meet
With actors, poets, lovers, friends and foes.
I felt uneasy, knowing some of those
Work and pleasure rivals would be quick
To exercise their wit and rhetoric
If my enormous overcoat seemed weird,
As I thought likely. I need not have feared.

Three people spoke of it, and all expressed
Surprise at seeing me so swishly dressed.
One, a younger man than I, a Beat
Poet from the wilds of Charlotte Street,
Begged with passion to discover where
I'd found it and he offered then and there
To buy it, throwing in his own coat free.
I was in step with fashion then. I see
In this small tale a little allegory,
A kind of metaphor for things apart
From those sartorial: for poetry, for art.

The old coat was discarded years ago.
My clothes are out of fashion now, although
I sometimes think that, if I keep them so,
Perhaps the time will come around when they
Again seem up to date. But I must say
This seems unlikely. Could anyone suppose
A craze for doublet and cross-gartered hose?
Impossible. But then, one never knows.

Poetic Encounters

The first poem to thrill and resound
in his skull and finger his senses,
awakening, too, a curious
and pleasurable sadness,
was called *He Fell Among Thieves*.
Its author was Sir Henry Newbolt.

Odd that a ten-year-old boy, living
in a bleak street of squinting dwellings
with shit-houses in the small back-yards,
should have been moved and haunted
by images of School Close
and Chapel, morning rides with father.

Not so odd that the second poem
to beguile him was Masefield's *Cargoes*,
that dance of rich flavours and colours,
tang and tingle of contrast.
For years he thought 'quinquereme'
was the name of an exotic fruit.

Now, knowing differently does not rob
the quinquereme of juice and fragrance
but increases the heft of the word;
and that yearning memory
of the never-known good place
still stirs in the wake of the poem.

Poet Tree

Until he reached the age of nine or ten
He lived in places north of Birmingham,
At first in Beeston, Nottinghamshire, and then
In Eccles, Lancashire, where he began
At school to learn by heart the wizard words
That, he was told, were known as 'poitry',
Words that soared and swooped and sang like birds,
Or rumbled in the dark mysteriously.

The vowel in 'poitry' rhymed, of course, with 'boy'.
Next, the family moved south, a place
Not far from London where they might enjoy
A better life – though this proved not the case –
And here at school he heard an alien sound:
The teacher spoke of 'poetry', the first
Syllable rhymed with cockney 'dough'. He found
His mind befogged, but then the mist dispersed.

Suddenly he saw the marvellous thing
Quite plain in silvery sunlight, tall, serene
Against blue sky, its branches blossoming
In multicoloured vocables from green
Syllabic buds, the flowering Poet Tree,
Where for centuries fabled birds had sung,
And under whose protecting canopy
Poets had dreamed, or from its branches swung.

A Binyon Opinion

They went with songs to the battle, they were young,
Straight of limb, true of eye, steady and aglow.
They were staunch to the end against odds uncounted,
They fell with their faces to the foe.

They shall not grow old, as we that are left grow old'

Laurence Binyon, *For the Fallen*

I was there, at Wipers and the Somme.
I left one leg at some place near Cambrai
And counted myself lucky, not like Tom,
My pal, what I won't see till Judgement Day.

So when this civvy poet says they 'fell
With faces to the foe' it don't sound right.
My pal, he never fell. A Jerry shell
Smashed him up to smithereens that night.

Another thing he says that's far from true:
That they – and he means us – was 'straight of limb'.
But half of our platoon, I swear to you,
Had bandy legs and wasn't tall and slim.

He says – and he means Tom and all those poor
Lads that got wiped out – 'they won't grow old',
As if it's something to be thankful for.
They ain't no Peter Pans. They're muck and mould.

They're dead, and Death's 'august and royal'
This poet claims. In civvy street maybe
It looks like that. These fibs make my blood boil.
Tom's dead and I'm alive – well, most of me.

November 11th 1997

Again the grey survivors try to call
Back from the dark the dead who now have lain
Too long in heedless dust to entertain
Much hope of resurrection in this Fall.
The damp and jaundiced leaves will soften all
The studded noise of marching feet. The stain
Of crimson on the gauze of mist and rain
Will never lure them from their vaulted hall.

I see two friends as they were long ago,
Images the heaped years can't displace,
Bill Gray whose guts were splattered in the snow,
Jim Rennie, picked off by a sniper's shot.
At least they have escaped what we now face:
You'd think this might console, but it does not.

Word Games

Things we utter without thinking,
as we chatter while we're drinking
or companionably strolling
through the meadows and the rolling
hills of favourite country walks,
sometimes, or you might say fairly
often, carry meanings rarely
thought of by the casual speaker,
meanings odder, maybe bleaker,
than belong in easy talks.

Phrases such as 'hit or miss'
could mean 'musical success
or unmarried lady'. Also
'hit' could signify a blow
with wielded weapon or a punch,
and 'miss' mean when the knuckly bunch
fails to find the aimed-at nose.

Depending largely on the context,
elementary terms have quite vexed
listeners with receivers tuned to
other stations: 'bats and balls' you
might think unambiguous,
but 'bats' could be small belfry-haunters
linked, improbably, with dancers –
a bit far-fetched, it's true.

'Pros and cons' would make most Majors
think at once of golf-instructors
in the company of jailbirds,
while other-ranks could see some ladies
of the night involved in scams.
Bookish people might have reason,
hearing that well-known expression
'nick of time', to think of Auden's
'prison of his days' where free men
are instructed 'how to praise'.

But enough of double meanings
though, for all of you with leanings
to the lexically ludic,
I'll leave, to see how you might view it,
'tit for tat', a common phrase,
like to provoke a titter,
though not perhaps among the liter-
ati, those whose brows might rise
just a little higher than ever.
So now I'll leave these words for you:
'tit for tat', and toodle-oo.

Losing Weight

It is something you have long desired.
Tired of lugging your load of fat
that blankets bone, tired of going slow,
you yearn to wear leanness, ache to amaze
your friends, enrage fat foes and plump wife:
life would be a lot better like that,
batter-pudding belly gone for good,
handsome, muscular, sleek as a cat.
But wait! This must be understood:

you can't expect your pectorals to swell
a steel cuirass, nor stomach ape
washboard corrugations, biceps and triceps
ripple and bulge, weight-lifter's thighs,
the waist of a supple dancer of tangoes;
too late, alas, by far, for those.

Maybe better, after all, to walk
stout and slowly on the shorter route,
unseductive and resigned
to being outpaced and scorned by the slender,
but not yet in immediate danger
of stripping down to the moon-white bone
the undiscriminating denizens of earth
will welcome to their dark, well-furnished home.

Premature Ejaculations

'Oh, goodness me!' he cried, and, 'Oh my word!'
Though nothing whatsoever had occurred.

Mummy

You stand at the window, mummy,
In the picture I have of you
With your permanent wave and your cupid's bow lips
And frock with waistline hugging your hips
And your eyes of such deep-sea blue.

No wonder the whole world loved you
And the beaux lined up to woo.
You looked like a movie star,
I'd have paid for a seat to watch you eat
The hearts they served up for you.

But what was it made you choose
The man with the Aryan nose
And big black coat and a hook of steel
Instead of a hand, and an iron mouth
That chomped and swallowed you?

But I could make him spew.
He just had to look at me,
And that's what he did, he up-threw,
And you were as good as new,
Once I'd mopped all the goo off of you.

Mummy, you're looking good now,
All I want is you.
We've got rid of the shit in the bottomless pit
And now it's just me and you.
Mummy, mummy, you darling, it's true.

Book of Days

At first, each day is blank, anonymous,
until you write or print or paint on it:
an empty page, of course quite meaningless.

Before you see the baker's shop is shut,
and hear church-bells and sniff the sizzling roast,
you wouldn't know which day you're looking at.

The click and whisper of the morning post,
or telephone's soft rasp, might start a new
twist in story-line and change the gist

of yesterday's account, then lead you to
territory you've never seen before,
that might, or might not, please and welcome you.

No one really knows what lies in store,
whatever calendars and stars may say;
but, if you hear a knocking at the door,

and irritably bawl out, 'Go away!'
it's yours to choose: your caller might have been
a long-limbed lovely who had come to stay,

or pale Jehovah's Witness with a clean-
cut countenance and drab but well-pressed suit,
or someone out of nightmare with a gun.

The girl, though, might have picked up some acute
sexually-transmitted sickness, while
the bible-tout could be the one who'd shoot.

You never know your luck. You might compile
a great thick wad of days, or you might not;
either way they'll tell a kind of tale

though, long or short, it won't contain a plot;
no dénouement, of course, where there's no knot.

Content and Discontent

I sit at the kitchen table, lunch finished;
rain whispers at the window; pale asterisks
splash against the pane, then vanish.

Pascal Rogé, on the 'wireless' as I still call it,
performs Ravel's *Concerto for Piano Left Hand*:
bright notes swarm from his clever mitt.

This work was commissioned by Paul Wittgenstein,
who gave his good right arm for the Fatherland,
a brave as well as a gifted man.

Open, on the table next to my side-plate,
is Frances Partridge's *A Pacifist's War*,
diaries kept during the second Big Fight

against the Germans from 1939
to '45, and on the plate can be seen
what is left of a Spice Pippin core.

It is many months since I wrote a poem.
Once, I might have been moved to write about
Wittgenstein's laying down of one arm

and his subsequent defiance and glory;
or something on music and the Second World War,
or even choose to celebrate once more

the taste and shape and mythopoeic power
of apples, their beauty and sheer appleness;
but I've tried all these before.

Music and apples, love, sacrifice and war –
all done with. It seems that I have quite run out
of things to write about;

except, maybe, this bankruptcy could offer
something in the way of subject-matter.
And it does: not much, though, to write home about.

Views and Distances

They sit together on their stolen towel
and count their few remaining francs and days
of dear vacation. Out in the bay the sea,
a crinkled spread of shimmering blue, sustains
an elegant white yacht at anchor there,
and, as they gaze, they see that, on the deck,
a man and woman have appeared who lean
languid at the vessel's rail and seem,
improbably, to offer stare for stare.

At night the sky's dark blue is deeper still,
is almost black. The rigging of the yacht
is hung with fairy-lights, and music drifts
and scents the air. The man in his white tux
and woman in her Dior gown still seem
to peer towards the shore as if they might
see once more the morning's teasing sight –
the enviable simplicities of youth
and deprivation, envy, appetite.

Some Times

'Time will tell,' said his grannie,
So he asked her what it would say;
But all she would tell him was: 'Quite a lot,
As you will find out one day.'

'Time flies,' his mother murmured.
'Where does it fly to?' he said.
'Over the mountains and over the seas.
Now off you go to bed.'

'I'm beating time,' said his father,
As he tapped his foot in the sun.
But the music stopped, and the band went home,
And time it was that won.

Silence

Defined as absence of all sound, and yet
a presence, ubiquitous and positive,
a necessary palimpsest to give
white space for various musics to be set
with words and other signs – the cryptic fret
of abstract traceries in time, a sieve
in which we separate the sparkling, live
birdsong from the glinting barrel's threat.

It is never absolute, not while the heart's
diastole and systole persist,
and human expirations mime the arts
of zephyrs waking leaves' green speech, and mist
the glass that shows who stays and who departs;
not while the pulse beats in the tender wrist.

Dead Stars

Last night I thought again of all the stars –
I don't mean those that prink the midnight sky,
which clever guys with telescopes can parse
and analyse and coolly classify –
not Sirius, the brightest of them all,
red giant or white dwarf, nor heads of pins
that pricked romantic skies we all recall
from tales in which the young prince always wins.

No, I thought of Gable, Stewart, Flynn,
Bogart, Tracy, Cooper and John Wayne;
thought, also, of those heavenly bodies in
their skin-tight velvet, Crawford and Fontaine,
Dietrich, Ava Gardner, Alice Faye,
still glowing in the dark, light years away.

Sestina of Sunday Music

Another Sunday evening; darkness falls
earlier now each day and I have drawn
the curtains long ago. Faint, distant calls
of nameless creatures pencil their forlorn
needs on silence's soft slate. Dry leaves
outside converse in whispers. A thin wind grieves.

Inside, a different kind of music grieves:
a measured threnody unfolds and falls
in melting pearls that form a pool which leaves
rich sonic fragrance in the air. Then, drawn
from woodwinds' lamentations and forlorn
complaints of strings, float wraiths of bugle-calls.

This is the Sunday music that recalls
dim images of loss and one who grieves
and gazes over moorland more forlorn
than twilit fields of crosses. Here rain falls
unceasingly. Gun-carriages, horse-drawn,
move with small thunder muffled by moist leaves.

It is not only genius that leaves
its legacy of melody which calls
our hearts to mastering heel where they are drawn
to passionate compliance: Rudolfo grieves
as poignantly as Dido. Waterfalls
of richness drench, but leave us still forlorn.

Whoever writes the score, the same forlorn
message is received. The years, like leaves,
are heaped beneath the trees; the last one falls,
and then the man in sable clothing calls.
Love can't be weighed by how the widow grieves.
Like all the hard-fought contests this is drawn.

Violins are beautiful as objects drawn
by master draughtsmen; even the forlorn
stone-or-tone-deaf solitary who grieves
apart perceives the sweep of sound that leaves
shapes of unuttered song, and so he calls
'Encore!' before the final curtain falls.

Then he, too, falls. The orchestra's withdrawn
and no more curtain-calls; the drained, forlorn
audience leaves, and darkening silence grieves.

Sunt Lacrimae Rerum

The glittering dance of brilliants must be strung
On that dark thread of sadness which is time,
No matter what bright melodies are sung.

When great symphonic combers swell and climb
Then curl and, swooping, rush towards the shore,
We hear a faint and melancholy chime.

This might come from a drowned cathedral or
Be carried on the wind from inland tower
In market-place, or church on distant moor.

Beneath the surging glory and the power
Of Beethoven or Bach, or tenderness
Of Schubert lieder's frailer sonic flower

We hear the spectral sighing of distress,
For time is music's element and we
Know murderous time can offer no redress.

Yet which of us, I wonder, were he free
To choose, would wish away the voice that sings
The keening descant of mortality

Inseparable from all that music brings
Of love, heart-piercing truth, the tears in things.

**Of Love
and War**

Baptism of Fire

He is no kid. He's nineteen and he's tough,
a hard man like Maclaren who, it's true,
is getting on in years and has three stripes,
and three kids, too, at home in civvy street;
but Sergeant Mac's a tough guy through and through:
he'll see them right when things get really rough.

They reach the starting-line in night's disguise.
It isn't fear exactly that he feels:
excitement, certainly, and something else,
a small black living thing inside his gut
that grows and squirms as sudden livid weals
are slashed across the dark face of the skies.

And, with the flashes, swollen thunder roars
as, from behind, the barrage of big guns
begins to batter credence with its din
and, overhead, death whinnies for its feed
while countering artillery shakes and stuns
with slamming of a million massive doors.

The iron fever of machine-gun fire –
more intimate but no less menacing –
spits tracers through the dark; his teeth begin
to chatter in spontaneous mimicry.
Flares' phosphorescent dahlias climb and cling.
His Company moves forward to the wire.

Beyond the wire the sand is sown with mines,
but Sappers have been there to cut a track
of safety through that zone of murderous tricks,
though if death doesn't burst from underfoot
it whistles through the air and can attack
from any angle and at any time.

Now shells and mortar-bombs explode around
and hurl dry geysers of detritus high;
he smells and tastes the fierce sweet bitterness
of cordite's pagan incense, then he hears
not far ahead, through mangled air, a cry –
a frail, yet weirdly penetrating sound:

at first unrecognised and meaningless,
a wordless wail, and then crude parody
of Sergeant Mick Maclaren's normal voice,
or what the voice might sound like if the man
were gelded or flung back to infancy,
a querulous sound of babyish distress.

Then words emerge: 'Oh mother! Mother! Please!
Oh Jesus Christ! Oh ma!' Grotesque, obscene.
After the first bewildering shock he feels
vicarious shame, a sense, too, of betrayal.
And then a shell's explosion intervenes:
blast knocks him grovelling to his contrite knees.

That voice has died away but echoes stain
a corner of his brain as others cry
for stretcher-bearers or God's aid, while he
is quite alone and lost, as they all are.
Old men at breakfast might know where and why
he's where he is – it's called El Alamein.

The Final Run

Huddled in his perspex world he sees
the other, night-swathed, world fall far below
and feels the engines of the Lancaster
settle to their steady humming drone
as, on the intercom, he hears the wheeze
and crackle of the static, then the cool,
smart-blazered public school tones of the skipper
checking on each member of the crew:
'Pilot to rear-gunner: all okay?'
He answers, 'Okay Skipper,' as he grips
the trips that swing his turret to and fro
from one side to the other, high and low,
quartering the sky in anxious search
for bristling predators, the Messerschmitts
and Junkers that could smash them from their perch
on shifty air and make their final run
the last indeed.
      This is his thirtieth raid
and then no more. Six months on cosy ground,
a cushy job instructing rookies, then,
with luck, the war would be kaput and he
need never suffer this ordeal again.

His final run: he shivers in his sweat
and, rising, peers below to see the faint
pale thread of surf that marks the Belgian coast
and knows ack-ack will soon begin to vent
its vivid rage in pyrotechnic show
of shells and tracers he has seen before
so many times and, minutes later, those
black branches far beneath begin to flower
in brilliant blossomings that flash and blaze.
He speaks into his mike; his throat is sore,
tongue thick with thirst: 'Gunner to pilot. Flak –
starboard quarter down!'

He feels his seat
fall away beneath him as the plane
dives and for a moment leaves him there,
breathless and suspended in the air,
before it levels and soars up again,
re-seating him, and then gets back on course.

The lethal firework show is left behind
and moonless night is smeared across his sight.
He stares into the murk and hopes to find
no moving menace there of any kind,
but almost instantly he is aware
of something flicking, quicker than a tick,
across his stare. It disappears, then zooms
distinctly into view – the vicious, slick
and hammer-headed Junkers 88
moving in to kill – and for one sick,
engulfing second he, and he alone,
is quivering, mortal target for that flight
of stinging tracers which he knows will soon
whizz sizzling through the night, all aiming for
his heartjammed, throbbing throat.
                                    His voice is hoarse:
'One Jerry fighter! starboard quarter down!
One thousand yards – prepare to corkscrew soon!'
                                    Death closes in,
expelling its thin stream
of evil brilliants as the gunner roars,
'Eight hundred yards!...now six!...five hundred!... –
Go!'
and presses his own triggers, sees the foe
bank and twist and slide away below
to leave the sky impassive as before.
He gasps out, 'Break away!'
                                    The pilot's voice
replies, 'Good lad, but keep a sharp lookout.
He might be back again.'
                                    And on they drone

until they are again saluted by
the flash and crack of ack-ack fire and fierce
blades of probing light thrust up to pierce
the scarred and trembling fabric of the night.
The plane is shaken, bounced, but on it flies
above the stricken city lit by fires
from earlier bombs. 'We're over target now!'
Bomb-aimer's voice: 'Left!...Steady!...Left again
and steady!...Bombs away! Okay!...Okay!...
Steady for incendiaries...they're gone!...
Let's get the hell away from here! Let's run!'

The aircraft with its quivering cargo veers
away to starboard, turns and heads for home.
The gunner stares through perspex at the crazed
astronomy of searchlight dazzle, flares
and tracers, shellbursts and infernal glow
from razed and burning buildings down below
and prays no fighters will swoop into view
to make the 'final' of their final trip
irreversibly and mercilessly true.
'For Christ's sake don't relax. We've come too far
to get the chop tonight!' The skipper's voice
is less urbane, democratised by fear.
The gunner grins but knows that his own voice,
should he speak now, would be as strained and hoarse,
if not far worse.
                              And then the aircraft bucks
and lurches as the blast from shellburst lifts
it tilting for long seconds and he hears
quick shrapnel rattle on the fuselage
and knows their corporate terror will not brook
denial or attempts at camouflage,
and all the crew is muttering spells or prayers.
                              And they survive.
The Lancaster drones on beyond the reach
of anti-aircraft fire, the naked flares
and questing jets of incandescent light.

Their target's crematorial glow recedes
and dims before it's swallowed by their flight.
Below, land melts away, becomes the sea,
and then the gunner dares, almost, to say
that they will make it, though he's often heard
grim tales of aircraft shot down close to base.
His throat is swollen now, his tongue warm-furred
and eyes feel like hot cinders, vision blurred.
The pilot speaks: his smooth tones, now restored,
sound casual and confident again:
'All right rear-gunner? Are you still awake?'

The plane is circling now. The gunner's grin
comes slow but wide: 'I'm fine. A piece of cake!'

Remembering the Dead at Wadi Akarit

The Millennium slithers to its close. A haggard December
damages the daylight; the bruised sky lours,
then darkness drapes the town though, in the Square,
the patient clock denies that this is night.

The old man gazes through an upstairs window-pane
over polished tiles and lemon lozenges of light
to where the town becomes an orange-tinted glow
against the sky. Thunder mutters like an afterthought.

This rumbling, though, reminds his mouth and throat
of a sharp, blue bitter-sweetness in stunned air
and slips a still-fresh picture in the window frame,
replacing the orange-smeared darkness there.

He sees the shapes of rock, the sand and rubble
on which, at unshaven dawn, the bodies sprawl
or lie with unpurposed and tidy decorum,
all neat in battle-order and KD uniform.

Disposed in their scattered dozens like fragments
of a smashed whole, each human particle
is almost identical, rhyming in shape and pigment,
all, in their mute eloquence, oddly beautiful.

As the sun strengthens, a faint sweet feculence spreads.
Dark birds wheel and soar. Fresh light applies
a maquillage of ochre and red. Furtive needs
and greeds begin to plunder the submissive dead.

The old man's eyelids flutter. He shakes his head.
The picture holds, then fades and slowly disappears
with cordite-breath and the pungent sweetness of the dead.
What stays is the shade of the unforgiving years.

Robbie

They all had a job to do in the platoon:
Mortar, rifle, One and Two on the Bren,
Or Section Leader with the light and lucky Sten.
But they also had their other parts to play:
Each of them chose a special role to act –
Walker, a gormless youth; Bill Gray, the buffoon;
Gordon Rennie, the world's pet uncle; Micky Rae,
A slash-lipped gangster; Davis, the rebel who attacked
All stout authority behind its Sam-Browned back.
Robbie alone played no part but his own:
Cotton-haired, potato-faced, he couldn't even say
What time it was; impossible to tell
How much he felt. Too dumb to act the clown,
With eyes like two dud flashlamp bulbs
He grinned a lot, seemed happy as a rule.

Near Caen, the day before the big attack,
Davis was heard to mutter to Bill Gray,
'Robbie's the lucky one who's not scared stiff.
He'll be all right. He can't tell night from day.
He's less imagination than my pack.
I envy him, I don't mind telling you.'
And Bill agreed. That night they got pinned down
By Moaning Minnies. Seven at a time
Those mortar bombs howled over, all night through.
It seemed impossible that anyone would live
But when the morning came things weren't too bad.
They checked their losses – only three were dead,
Among them Robbie. Clever for once, he had
Sucked on his rifle-muzzle like a straw
And somehow blown away most of his head.

Love and Courage

When Barnes, the beefy bully, ambushed him
while crossing Casey's Field that afternoon
heading from school for home's safe certainty,
he howled for pity, but was given none.
The pain he felt was nothing to the shame
of weak submission he was dirtied by.
Fear paralysed; he couldn't even run.

Ten years later, when war's thunder rolled
and cloud-sacks spilled fierce hail of fire and steel,
he was compelled to put on uniform
and learn to dish out death. He could conceal
his terror till his Company was called
to face real battle's homicidal storm.
He chose desertion, ignominy and jail.

That is, if choice existed, which I doubt.
When nervous 'peace' was finally restored
he was released, but still found much to fear.
If accident or argument occurred
in street or square he quickly turned about
and walked the other way. Yet he'd declare
the charge of cowardice to be absurd.

His conduct was determined, he maintained,
by what he was – imaginative, kind,
and sensitive. His nature, never made
for deeds of derring-do, had been designed
for art and tenderness. Yet, in the end,
he failed there, too; for love and courage need
the selfless heart, by which both are defined.

Old Wounds

Long ago the wounds were healed,
and he forgets that they once bled
and burned and blotted out the light
and sumptuous colours of the world,
and filled his unprotected head
with loud but wordless night.

Now each wound quietly lies below
its dark or silver cicatrice
and does not hurt at all, unless
the weather turns and bleak winds blow
with threats, or their fulfilment, of
unpitying hail and snow.

Then pain, or its pale phantom, haunts
the places where it left its prints;
but other kinds of hurt occur:
a half-forgotten tune or scent
can penetrate, and slyly stir
long dormant shades of her.

As when, two days ago, he saw
her cross the street; and there she stood,
her smile against the sun, half-frown,
a look that he had always loved.
Then she was gone. The wound wept raw,
and words seeped out like blood.

Love

Is it like a carnival with spangles and balloons,
Fancy-dress and comic masks and sun-drenched afternoons
Without a cloud to spoil the blue perfection of the skies?
'Well yes, at first, but later on it might seem otherwise.'

Is it like a summer night when stock and roses stain
The silken dark with fragrance and the nightingale again
Sweetly pierces silence with its silver blades of song?
'I say once more it can be thus, but not for very long.'

Is it like a great parade with drums and marching feet
And everybody cheering them, and dancing in the street,
With laughter swirling all around and only tears of joy?
'If that alone, you'd find the fun would soon begin to cloy.'

Is it like the falling snow, noiseless through the night;
Mysterious as moonlight and innocent and bright,
Changing the familiar world with its hypnotic spell?
'It has been known to be like that, and other things as well.

'But if you find, when all the brightest ribbons have grown frayed,
The colours faded, music dumb, and all that great parade
Dismissed into the darkness where the moon has been put out,
Together you find warmth and strength, then that's what it's about.'

Why?

They ask me why I love my love. I say,
'Why do summer's roses smell so sweet
And punctually put on their rich display?

'Why does winter lash the fields with sleet
And make cold music in the leafless trees
Yet strangely seem to warm our snug retreat?

'Why does moody April taunt and tease
With alternating sun and dancing rain?
Why do nettles sting the flesh like bees?

'Why are the stars tonight like silver grain
Broadcast on the far dark fields of sky?
Why does the owl rehearse its sad refrain?

'With loving, too: no point in asking why.
There is no answer.' That is my reply.

The Power of Love

It can alter things:
The stormy scowl can become
Suddenly a smile.

The knuckly bunched fist
May open like a flower,
Tender a caress.

Beneath its bright warmth
Black ice of suspicion melts;
Danger is dazzled.

A plain and dull face
Astounds with its radiance
And sudden beauty.

Ordinary things –
Teacups, spoons and sugar-lumps –
Become magical.

The locked door opens;
Inside are leaves and moonlight;
You are welcomed in.

Its delicate strength
Can lift the heaviest heart
And snap hostile steel.

It gives eloquence
To the dumb tongue, makes plain speech
Blaze like poetry.

Summer in the Park

Sun leans lightly on all temples;
In the park the far trees
Melt at their shadowed knees.
Summer supplies its simples
For all but one disease:
Young dogs, young sons, young mothers,
Gold waterfall hair of daughters
Float over trim green seas.
He could munch them up and swallow them,
Yes, even the melting trees,
The staid man on the seat
Whose heart's teeth ache with love
And its impossible sweet.

Desirable Residence

They came quick stepping, laughing lively,
Loving hands held warm and tightly;
Their eyes were ripe and bright,
And both were handsome in their light
Suits of youth. Her walk was dance
And his quick march.
They mocked the staid with stance and glance,
And then they paused outside the house,
Admired its pretty clothes,
The shine and sparkle and the green
Apron fringed with rose.
Each faced the other, smiled, and then,
Still holding hands, clicked smartly in;
And they were never seen again.

Questions about Paradise

Did it rain in the Garden of Eden?
Did original man and his mate
improvise leafy umbrellas
and wait for the storm to abate?

Was it chilly at night in the Garden?
Did they shiver with cold as they lay
huddled together in bracken,
longing for temperate day?

And what did they have for their breakfast?
What would Eve rustle up there to eat?
It wouldn't be kidneys or bacon
for they neither, surely, ate meat.

They might have drunk something like coffee
or tea but, more probably milk.
They didn't wear clothes for adornment
or warmth, neither cotton nor silk.

Did they fuck before eating the apple?
The Bible on this isn't clear;
they certainly did after sentence
or else you and I'd not be here.

But how did they talk to each other,
to God and the serpent as well?
They must have commanded a language
to speak with, if not write and spell.

It is true that the word 'prelapsarian'
connotes a past heavenly state,
yet it seems that those two vegetarian
nudists chose outside the Gate.

For while they were stuck in the Garden,
life surely was terribly bleak,
just the two with so little to talk of,
if indeed they were able to speak.

Their lives were devoid of all passion
and contrast and music and art,
ignorant of love and the secret
dark galleries deep in the heart.

It was Eve, with her feminine instinct
for the basics, who well understood
to be human you have to discover
the nature of evil and good,

and that beauty, love and fulfilment
are conditional, not dished out free,
contingent on time and on hazard,
and on Death's stern necessity.

Five Versions of Rimbaud

I: *Ophelia*

On the tranquil black river where dreaming stars rest
Ophelia floats slowly, liliaceously pale
On her long wavering veils; from the woods in the west
Sound the horn-notes of hunters saluting their kill.

For more than a thousand sad years she has drifted,
white phantom afloat on the endless dark river,
and all through that time her sweet madness has whispered
its tale to the breeze-troubled willows that shiver.

The amorous wind is caressing her bosom
and it gently unfolds her white veils in a wreath
that lifts and subsides to the river's slow rhythm;
the willows arch over and weep out their grief.

Water-lilies also draw close and are sighing,
and sometimes her passing elicits from leaves
brief flutter of wings discreetly applauding
the shimmering music the night sky achieves.

*

O pale Ophelia, beautiful as snow,
you died and were borne by the river away;
it was winds from the white peaks of Norway that brought you
both the message of freedom and the price you must pay.

And the wind in your hair breathed those rumours that stirred
such dark perturbations of spirit and mind;
your tender heart listened to Nature and heard
the night's trembling sigh and the great trees that groaned.

It was the roar of the lunatic ocean that broke
your vulnerable spirit, soft heart of a child;
and the poor mad prince who, unable to speak
on that morning in April, saw you beguiled.

What a rich dream of love and freedom, mad girl!
He was the fire, and you melted like snow;
your vision's great glory choked back all the words;
infinity dazzled and stunned like a blow.

*

And the poet has told us that now you come seeking
by starlight the flowers you once gathered with care;
and again he has seen, in her long veils reclining,
the lily Ophelia, still beautiful there.

*

II: *A Winter Dream*

In winter we'll ride in a small railway carriage
            with pink decor and cushions of blue;
in each cosy corner a nest of wild kisses
            to be plundered by me and by you.

You will close your bright eyes against prowling shadows
            that bring, in the darkness, vile shapes,
which, glaring and snarling, press close to the windows,
            monsters that no one escapes.

Then, light as a spider, my delicate kisses
will tickle your cheek like an insect that passes
            on to your neck where you'll feel

its journeying downwards. 'Oh help! I beseech you!'
you'll cry as, together, we search for this creature
            well-known for exploratory zeal.

III: *The First Evening*

She was half-dressed, or less than half.
Great voyeuristic trees outside
pressed their leaves against the glass,
slyly pushing, spreading wide.

Half-naked in my chair's embrace
she sat, with both hands clasped together.
Her little feet showed such sweet grace,
trembling on the floor with pleasure.

I saw a little beam of light,
waxen-tinted, playing over
her smiling lips and on the white
curve of breast, a fly on roses.

I kissed her dainty ankles. She
laughed, at first a soft low note
which then rose bright and trillingly,
crystalline from her arched throat.

Her small feet hid beneath frail tent
of petticoat. 'Do stop!' she cried,
her laugh pretended punishment
for what in fact she had desired.

I softly kissed her trembling eyes
that fluttered under my warm lips.
She moved her head away and sighed:
'I think this far enough, perhaps...

'I've things to say, so listen sir...'
I moved my lips from eyes to breast,
and, as I kissed and fondled her,
her throaty laugh held no protest.

She was half-dressed, or less than half.
Great voyeuristic trees outside
pressed their leaves against the glass,
slyly pushing, spreading wide.

IV: *The Lice Hunters*

When the child's head is tortured by red
malice of lice, he yearns for the white
calm solace of dreams, but now in its stead
come his two lovely sisters, nails silvery bright.

They seat him in front of the wide open casement
where blue air is scented by cocktails of flowers
and the night-dew descends, anointing his opulent
locks where their fingers are magical prowlers.

He hears the soft sighs of their vigilant breathing
which carries the honey-sweet fragrance of roses,
broken at times by a salivary hissing
from lips moist for kissing, a sound that bemuses.

He can hear, too, their eyelashes beat in the silence
like dark wings of insects; he feels their slim fingers,
electrically thrilling, passing death-sentence;
hears tiny explosions, minikin angers.

And then the child feels a deep languor steal over
all senses, a cloaking melodious sigh;
those fingers, caressing, induce a strange fever,
mysterious tristesse, a compulsion to cry.

V: The Sleeper in the Valley

A grassy hollow with a lilting river
which scatters its silvery shreds on the reeds
as the sun from the hills sets the calm air aquiver
with shimmering light that floods and recedes:

a young and bare-headed soldier sleeps there;
his lips are apart, cress cool on the skin
of vulnerable neck; he lies in the glare
and waterless drizzle of afternoon sun.

His feet in the tall yellow irises rest
and he smiles like a child at his mother's soft breast;
O, cradle him gently in arms warm and wide.

He is cold and his delicate nostrils are closed
to sonatas of fragrance that Summer's composed.
Two crimson holes have been punched in his side.

The Year of the Crab

Intimations of Mortality

In fading English summer where, quite soon,
the wistful autumn would begin its fall
before the winter bared its moon-white fangs,
he planned escape from winds that pierce and hurt:
he booked a flight to a winterless land
of speedwell sky and vanilla sand.
Already, though, a vague discomfort stirred;
pain's pallid shadow and its soundless trill
flickered in his throat.
                                The Doctor said
'It's thrush,' and gave him lozenges to suck.
The ache remained. Again, the same prescription,
but no change; slight darkening of the shade perhaps,
invading places other than the flesh.

Weeks sidled past; leaves crisped and floated down,
slithering in the soupy air. The ancient scents
of autumn bonfires came and went.
The Doctor frowned, more puzzled than alarmed,
and sent him to a specialist who found
no thrush had nested snug in his warm throat,
no feathered flutter, but the hard-clawed crab.

The plane for warm escape stayed on the ground.

....

The words were heard and understood:
no knife-blade shock. It seemed as if
some half-expected news had come at last.
And so the measured processes began
which brought him here, to winter and this bed,
where neutered and more neatly parcelled than
ever at home in longed-for, shared domain
of love and sleep, he looks around and sees

the so-far nameless others, like himself embossed
along the margins of the ward, each one a word,
synonymous, not quick or lumbering verb,
but each a hybrid vocable, half adjective, half noun,
a 'patient' – and, inertly patient, he
and ever one of them would have to be.

Choice, with their outdoor clothing, has been locked
            away.

He cannot move, except inside his head
where move he does, not far in time or space,
a few weeks only, travelling in reverse
to when he was escorted to the 'Mould Room' for
the fitting of his plastic 'shell', or 'mask'.
Warm bandages were wound about his head and neck
until his face was covered save for holes
cut out for eyes and mouth. He thought
that he must be a sight to terrify
the young or, to the old, bring images
in black and white of H.G. Wells's Man
beneath whose bandages were nothingness and night.

The cast of head and neck set hard;
from this the mask or shell was shaped.
Next came the X-rays, then the 'Simulation'
when radiotherapy's procedures were rehearsed:
they stretched him out on what they called the 'couch'
on which the glassy shell of plastic which contained
his captive head was firmly clamped,
immovable, beneath the engine's steady hum:
all music killed, all singing dumb,
frivolities of far-off pleasures drilled
by that thin driving sound. The plastic shell
became a world of glass, his skull
its sole inhabitant, fixed firm and still
as specimen in laboratory or museum.

After this the real thing could begin.

The Machine Room

This scene, to a neutrally cool gaze, might seem
like footage from an early film, Fritz Lang perhaps,
an unmade movie mixing modes –
a quasi-scientific vision of a world
in black and white, mysterious machines,
attended figures, sacerdotal, gowned,
and a horror film in which the home-made man
is yet to rise from where he lies, strapped down,
to set about his mad creators and rove wild.
But, to the patient in his vitreous world,
stretched on his trestle-bed, the room
is sounds of movement, mechanical and alive,
steely sighs and groans, a steady hum,
then conference of voices, low, intent,
discussing problems in their unknown tongue
while he, like his own grandchild, listens to
the serious grown-up sounds that make no sense.

Darkness and light perform their dance.
He counts masked seconds as they shuffle past
and waits for his release.
He prays that he will neither sneeze nor cough.

Then, with unexpected and explosive crash,
the plastic shell containing neck and head
is – as always, shockingly – unclamped,
and he is helped by practised hands
down from the narrow couch to stand
restored to a brief and dizzy perpendicular
before being lowered to his patient chair
and wheeled away towards the ward
to lie and wait until the following day's
confinement in the glassy cranial cell.

The Treatment

Day after aching day, week after clubfoot week,
the course of radiation moved
towards its fifth and final week;
and now, at last, the daily treatments done,
he wears a scarf of stinging-nettles
tight about his throat.
His mouth, a little dungeon, dark and dry,
is haunted by the vile, insistent shade
of putrefying fish; a slender tube
creeps up one nostril and descends
to unprotesting stomach to convey
some tasteless stuff that holds him down to earth.

He hears faint fluttering reports
of snow and early dark, and longs for her
to bring that perfect sweetness to the heart's
unsullied palate and the faint,
remembered fragrance of her wake.

Loving the Nurses

Slowly, the long pale bandage of each day
unwinds and darkens as the night descends;
hygienic and efficient hands bring opiates
and pain slinks off to its hot lair.
He feels for every nurse a blend
of gratitude and admiration that, together, ape
the lineaments of love; he has read somewhere
all patients fall in love with those who wear
the uniform of trained compassion; now he learns
that this is almost true, though 'almost' rules
with that authority which overturns
the absolute of 'true' as his true love
comes in from loveless night and bring those spoils
which neither he nor his affliction earns.

Night Shift

Well past midnight now: outside,
beyond these still curtains, heavy with implications,
their secretive corrugations,
the wind whimpers and whispers to be let in.

A single circular lamp, stunned moon,
flat on the ceiling, dilutes the dark
but cannot cancel it. The quietness
is never absolute; sleep crumples it.

The sighs and snarls of human breathing
seem no more meaningful than the wind's noise
or the faraway whispering of a nurse:
her voice is a tuneless lullaby.

At spaced intervals the figures move,
sexless in their long vague robes,
slow and soundless down the ward,
anonymous and self-absorbed.

The pale procession will last as long
as darkness lasts. They have lost
their ordinariness with their identities.
They are practising at being ghosts.

Morning Shift

After the gaunt night, its taut sheet
of silence torn from time to time
by sudden cries and the urgent morse

of hurrying feet, the hushed confabulations,
darkness clinging still to outer panes
behind the brooding curtains,

comes the time of neither night nor sunrise,
a brief, noiseless lacuna of exhaustion,
before the morning shift arrives,

not seen as yet, but audible,
an awakening of starlings and sparrows,
laughter, voices, the cold scent of dew and dawn,

a distant whisper of wind in shivering leaves,
a rumour of drenched petals unfolding:
morning puts on its fresh starched uniform.

Going Home

The daily dosages of radiation are now finished.
External and internal flesh of throat and neck
simmers with sores. The marvel, Morphine, holds
the pain away. He has not swallowed food or drink
for months; the nasogastric tube is still in place,
it trails, escaped spaghetti, from his nose
to be attached to feeding-pump four times each day.
His love learns from the nurses how to handle this,
what drugs and in what quantities to give,
and then he is released to leave for home
where all his nursing will be done
by unofficial care which, uncomplaining, works
on every shift with only gratitude for wage.

Although it takes stretched months
and two returns to hospital before
he can attempt to eat as others do,
the time draws slowly closer and, at last, he hears,
if only faintly, that low growl and purr
of powerful aero-engines, fuelled now
for long-delayed escape to winter warmth,
the land where orange-blossom stains soft air
when sleet and snow enshroud the fields of home,
a place of soft, slow rhythms, real Cockaigne
which not long since, in misery and pain,
he feared that he would never see again.

Postscript: Andalusian Afternoon

In the narrow street between the tall
white buildings with jet iron traceries
and whispered secrecies of glass,
which tell you nothing though they hint
at sensuous possibilities, dark shadows slant
and splash on wall and paving-stone. Two children
are laughing as they play with a large black dog
and a pink balloon, while he and she
look down, unseen, from their small balcony.

Behind them, still and cool, the room recalls
once more a Schubert Trio in B Flat
and, as the Scherzo dances, the black dog bounds
and pounces on the light pink globe
of air held tight in shining weightless skin
which quite astounds by bouncing free,
unpunctured by the canine claws,
and, teasing, settles only feet away.
Delighted squeals float up like small balloons.

And this slight incident, without intent,
is beautiful, this moment in a burnished afternoon
in a lofty room in Southern Spain
will be remembered with that nimble tune,
black glossiness of dog and pink balloon,
and if a whisper of uncertainty is heard
between the scherzo and the rondo it affords
a glint of seasoning, a piquancy,
which makes the mortal moment more their own.

Behind
the Lines

Aunt Clarice Dancing the Charleston

The motorway hazy, an evening in summer,
now twilit, the pause before swooping darkness;
headlamps approaching already aglimmer
but icily pale; incessant the sizzle
of tyres on the tarmac; at a touch the car radio
awakens to flavour the gaoled air with music,
saxophone, drums, piano and trumpet.

Tear-starred gaiety of prohibition ragtime
exhumes silky images of shimmying dancers,
the men in white tuxes or blazers and flannels,
the women in beaded dresses that shimmer,
shamelessly showing their silken patellas,
and I think, for the first time in years, of Aunt Clarice,
and see her in sepia, smiling in sunshine,
on the beach at Skegness, a foxtrotting 'flapper'
who never was wed, though, whenever she visited,
she arrived each time with a different 'uncle' –
or so it now seems – and with one she called Bowen
she danced the Charleston to a portable gramophone,
both of them huge in our trembling front parlour.

As a child I could sense that she did not much like me
and guessed her distaste encompassed all children.
In her smile there was something secret, unsharing,
something disturbing, beyond definition,
that carried a whiff, now just recognisable
as faintly corrupt, ambiguously sexual.

Years flickered past with no meeting or letter
till I, middle-aged, was told she was ailing,
ancient, deranged, and perhaps needing succour.
I went to her home in a North London suburb
and pressed on the doorbell. The person who answered,
an elderly nurse or companion, invited me
into the hall where I saw, on the staircase,
the crazed old woman who had once been Aunt Clarice,
the dancer of Charleston, collector of 'uncles',
now wild and dishevelled, shrieking a litany
of loathing and fear and abusive obscenities.
Her companion then thought it best I should leave.

Now twilight surrenders to night's massive presence,
the headlamps of all the oncoming traffic
are changed from pale lenses to wild glaring goggles;
like blobs of bright acid they burn through the blackness.
I switch off the radio, but not all the music
is silenced; I still hear the silvery echoes
of trumpet and saxophone, pulse of percussion,
beneath the tyres' sibilance and soft growl of engine,
as the beams of my own lights spear through the darkness,
which yields to my entry but closes behind me
on Clarice and Bowen as they dance the Charleston
in a terrible century's doomed adolescence.

Redolences

Glos: O, let me kiss that hand!
Lear: Let me wipe it first; it smells of mortality.

Those childhood whiffs, those pungencies
and fragrances, no longer known
except in memory,
still haunt this summer evening and they bring
related images of place and thing,
black jewels of tar on sun-stunned roads,
the creaking of a garden swing.

The garden darkens, and the scents
of honeysuckle, roses, stock,
persist. Though hidden now
from sensible cognition they remain
mysteriously present in the brain
to tease, then cunningly unlock
those little cells of zest and pain.

Sunlight, the yellow smell of hay
in Folly Lane; then counterpoint
of silage and manure;
outside the inn, the breath of various beers
from open door and windows commandeers
the air with whispers redolent
of grown-up secrets, hungers, fears.

Then other odours, not quite lost
to deft imagination's net
that trawls the populous past
for sweet and yeasty scents of hymns and bells,
the sooty reek of lachrymose farewells
as train-doors slam; though we forget,
with luck, that hand, and how it smells.

A Small Hunger

Ballaghadereen the place, in County Roscommon,
A time of horse-lugged wagons, vans and carts
On cobbled streets where children, men and women
Would gasp with goggling eyes and pounding hearts
To see the sky astonished to play host
To one frail, tilted, sputtering aircraft which
Swung on blue nothingness. Here, few could boast
A motor car, and nobody was rich.

I was four years old, my brother six.
We lived on tatties, fish and soda bread,
No luxuries, like buns or sugar sticks,
Except, perhaps, on birthdays. Mother said,
'Count your blessings. Others have far less.'
True, no doubt, but life for us was grim.
The Old Man doused all sparks of happiness;
Those 'others' didn't have to live with him.

Astounding now to think that he was then
No more than thirty years of age, and yet
He'd learnt already more than older men
Would know, or wish to know, of how to get
Enjoyable excitement from the pain
Of those to whom his name was synonym
For misery. We boys had often lain
In trembling dark, afraid, and hating him.

One early summer evening, back from work,
He called to us to come to him at once.
This time no glint of menace seemed to lurk
Beneath the urgency, a circumstance
Strange enough to puzzle us. We saw
His broad excited grin; his eyes were bright
With secret glee we'd rarely seen before,
A keen, anticipatory delight.

Our fear of him, though there, was modified
By curiosity. 'Come here,' he said,
'I've something for you, though I might decide
I'd rather keep it for myself instead.'
He held both hands behind his back. 'Guess what...
Come on! What can it be do you suppose?
It's yours if you can tell me what I've got!'
We shook our heads and whispered our 'Don't knows'.

A pause and then he grinned and said, 'All right,
I'll show it you. Now shut your eyes until
I say that you can look.' We closed them tight,
And waited in our darkness while the thrill
Of expectation almost overcame
Mistrust and apprehension. Then he spoke
And broke the silence with my brother's name.
'Take it!' he said. 'Go on! It's not a joke!'

In almost utter disbelief we stared
And saw him holding up, just out of reach,
A block of chocolate. 'Cadbury's,' he declared,
'The biggest size and you can have half each.'
Its blue and silver splendour dazzled us.
We gazed, amazed, and neither of us stirred.
'You want it, don't you? Well then – no or yes.
All you've got to do is say the word.'

We stayed quite still. He said, 'Be quick before
I change my mind!' And now his grin was crazed.
My brother took the chocolate slab and tore
The shining outer wrapper off and gazed
A moment at the silveriness revealed
Before he ripped the flimsy stuff away.
We saw then what the pretty wraps concealed –
A block of wood; a dummy for display.

We heard his wild, abandoned laughter skirl
and saw the demons jumping in his eyes.
My brother did not speak, nor did he hurl
The thing away. We could not find disguise
For disappointment, though we bit back tears.
What lay beneath deceitful wrappings teased
And floated on mad laughter down the years,
The ghost of a small hunger, unappeased.

Going Home

The light has softened from the noon's bright clamour
to a gentler tone as the evening steals
over the fields where you walk slowly home.
Hetta, your whippet, as light as a shadow,
follows at heel, and for a long moment
all sound is suppressed, a holding of breath,
suspension of thought, an unfurnished dream
or tabula rasa; then frail as a moth-wing,
source hidden by distance, no more than a whisper,
sound drifts from the river and over the meadows,
as wispy as thistledown, unseizable froth.

But now it grows stronger, is heard as a voice,
the voice of a woman, strange yet familiar,
calling the same sound, over and over;
it could be your name, the trochee repeated
beseeching six times before it is swallowed
by silence which leaves not the ghost of an echo.
And then the far murmur of traffic returning
and, nearer, the blackbird's fluting arietta
restore you and Hetta to terra cognita.
You step out more briskly, heading for home.

For less than ten seconds, perhaps, you felt young,
not happy exactly, but visited by
a phantom of rapture: the woman's voice floating
your name on the halcyon air of the evening,
calling you back to a place never known.

A Numinous Event

Only once in my life have I experienced
A numinous event. God spoke to me.
I do not mean this metaphorically
Or by dream or through Urim or a prophet
But that He spoke to me with a physical voice
Which issued from the mystery beyond
The dark sky and its white rash of stars
On a frosty night on Ealing Broadway.
I stood transfixed, amazed, my face raised
To feel a silvery beatitude descend.

I don't remember the exact words uttered
Nor could I honestly describe the voice
Except that I would swear that it was male.
But this I do recall with total certainty:
The tone was benevolent and reassuring.
Church bells began to roll and tremble in the skies
For it was Christmas Eve and all the pubs
Had extensions of their licenses.

I think God was forgiving me for my absence
From His mass. I know that He spoke to me.
Although the words themselves are lost
Or, if not lost, are hidden in the mist
Of almost half a century. And yes,
I must confess,
I might have been at least a little pissed.

Buttercups in Stormlight

Mid-June, and after five generous days
of gently fierce, unbridled sun,
the sky is plum-skin purple, tight and dark.

The air is clenched and motionless
under the undelivered tons
of thunder, yet translucent light is calm.

It is tinted, though, with mulberry.
How the quietness scents it, here by the slow river
where elderflower and cow-parsley are delicately bright.

Wild roses wrench the heart and senses,
yet nothing is so bewitching as these
clusters of familiar buttercups.

They are remade in this veiled, purple day,
luminous, so radiant, glossy, clean,
so yellow that all other yellows fade.

Bananas, custard, even daffodils
are something else less yellow than these small
and unassertive, shining buttercups

that now compel, enthral and hold
the unborn storm enraptured, so
it neglects its business and forgets to fall.

Legal Tender

'Brown's made of money!' These words puzzled me
when I first heard them at the age of seven,
spoken by my grumpy Uncle Stephen.
Like a snowman's made of snow? How could he be?

Money, to me, was clinking metal, round –
ha'pennies and pennies that could buy you sweets;
the silver coins for more expensive treats
were rarely seen and almost never owned.

Each Christmas Day, before I grew too old,
I'd find, in stocking or on Christmas tree,
a small net scarlet bag and you could see
it held a dozen coins of glittering gold.

The gold, of course, was bogus, made of thin
shining foil, and yet its gleam was more
exciting than the aspect real cash wore:
it hinted sweet delight beneath the skin.

Perhaps my Uncle's Mr. Brown was made
of dollar bills, a faceless lightweight guy.
Once, I'm told, in Borneo they'd buy
goods with human skulls, a grisly trade.

Not sinister, but every bit as strange
were feather-money in New Hebrides,
salt in Ethiopia, oxen in Greece;
all, long ago, were media of exchange.

Today, approaching the Millennium's close,
the paper and the clinking stuff is less
often used for trading, though I'd guess
more is stashed away than you'd suppose,

stored in little glittering hoards beneath
old mattresses and under creaking floors,
concealed in socks inside camphoric drawers
among old photos, hairpins and false teeth.

Although ignored, forgotten and unspent
they keep some shine, survive their savers who,
whatever they were made of, had to bow
before Time's final disembellishment.

Getting There

Away from the reek and hammering glare of this
loud thoroughfare where dangers lurk like mines
that smash incautious travellers to bits,
you would be wise to heed those little signs
that lead to lanes and byways where you'll find
not only relative safety but, with luck,
some calmer vistas which possess a kind
of power to kindle dreams the highways lack.

Not only in the countryside, of course,
but in the streets and alleys where you smell
sly fragrances whose dark evocatory source
lies in a time and place you once knew well
but suffered exile from; in ginnels, too,
where croodling pigeon-loft and Monday's wash
compose a statement eloquent as true;
there you can stroll, or linger if you wish.

But if you yearn to reach the great good place,
or even catch a glimpse of it one day,
you know you'll have to venture out to face
the hazards of the populous highway,
and in that fiercer light and space you must
confront the risks and strike out, or be struck,
be unafraid though vigilant, and trust
your vehicle, clear vision and pure luck.

The Journey: a Dialogue

What preparations did you have to make
for the journey that you chose to undertake?

Not many and quite simple: lots of plain
or lined A4, warm drinks that don't contain
soporific substances, and then,
of course, a pencil or some kind of pen –
whichever is the easier to use –
thick blinds for blotting out distracting views,
stout doors for solitude and quietness,
and any kind of comfortable dress.

Did you travel with a dragoman or friend
to offer help and guidance or extend
that welcome word of reassurance when
you might have missed the company of men?

I went alone, of course, as everyone
who's been on such a journey must have done.

And did your journey work out as you'd planned,
or was there snow where you expected sand?
To put it simply, did you lose your way,
or get waylaid, or somehow led astray
by sinuous temptations? Did you keep
steady on your course or fall asleep
when senses should have been alert and clear?
Did resolution fade, then disappear?

All of those, and none.

What do you mean?

I mean that, yes I sometimes found I'd been
led by ignis fatuus or plain
laziness down tracks to bleak terrain
that yielded nothing valuable to me.
But you must understand: there could not be
a plan or chart from which to deviate:
the senses were my compass; vade-mecum, fate.

And did you succeed? How did your journey end?

I found I was unable to contend
with all the twists and obstacles I met
on that long trek. I lost a lot of sweat
for no reward. I didn't ever find
an epiphanic goal of any kind.

What is it like, this place you tried to reach?
A glittering city? Solitary beach
with whispering wavelets fingering the sand?
A place of magic, kind of fairyland?
Primeval woods where innocent killers dwell?

I'll say it once again, so listen well:
I didn't reach it, so how am I to tell?

The Veteran's Advice

The thing you find may not be what you seek,
which doesn't mean it will be valueless;
the best approach is cautious and oblique.

At first you should have something more or less
specific in your sights – a place of shade,
perhaps, and dear remembered loveliness,

or precious keepsake carelessly mislaid –
but once the search is underway you must
forget whatever prudent plans you've made.

Let eyes and feet go walkabout and trust
the voice that whispers softly, though you may
begin to feel you're hopelessly nonplussed.

It's always best to go the longest way
to find what otherwise you might not spot,
though what that is, or might be, who can say?

Not I, or anyone, can tell you what.
Maybe the stars could say, and maybe not.

Behind the Lines

Small canvas town of bell-tents and marquees
which serve as dining-hall and wet canteen;
rough-laundered khaki shirts flap in the breeze
outside most tents, for here the men can clean
those grime-encrusted garments they have worn
for weeks in stinking dug-outs, day and night,
here where the fields are opulent with corn
and they can walk quite safely in plain sight.
Distance tames the menace of the guns;
the cries for stretcher-bearers reach the ears
only at night in sleep, where wounded sons,
unmanned, cry out for mother through their tears.
These fields are sown with poppies, not with mines;
no murderous snipers lurk behind the lines.

Evening, and the street lamps palely bloom
as curtained windows flush with warmth and light,
though in one high and skylit attic room
the naked glass admits incurious night
and, looking down, reflects the smooth dark face
of polished table-top on which a white
sheet of foolscap lies. The only trace
of human presence is the teasing sight
of writing – verse, it seems – too far away
to be deciphered, and a pen left there
to be picked up perhaps another day,
unless it was abandoned in despair
when this truth struck: the poem that sings and shines
lies bound and gagged, and locked behind the lines.

Questioning the Master

Tell me how to do it,
please tell me all you know.
I know you know the secret
that makes the whole thing flow.

Should I do it this way,
or should I do it that?
with a bottle-opener
or a cricket-bat?

I know you are an expert,
so tell me what to do,
how to go about it:
I'd do the same for you.

I've got a shining sabre,
ballet-dancer's tights,
an old Lee Enfield rifle
with telescopic sights,

a compass and a camera,
a fountain-pen and axe,
a truncheon and harmonica,
a symphony by Bax.

I've stocked up with provisions,
scotch eggs and acid drops,
a case of Irish whiskey
and frozen mutton chops.

So how do I get started?
Close both eyes and leap?
Wriggle slowly forward,
or first lie down and sleep

and hope oneiric vision
will set me on the way,
if not the following morning,
at least some time next day?

Why don't you answer, Master,
all the things I've said?
Oh Lord! I think he's sleeping
or, more than likely, dead.

It Should Be Easier

It should be easier after all these years
of concentrated effort, some success,
the audiences' silence, hoots or cheers,

the last infrequent, as you must confess,
but though they made rare music in your ears,
their absence never caused you real distress.

The old excitement, mix of hopes and fears,
has lost its kick, the impulse to return
for one more tussle fades as darkness nears.

And if you try again you only learn
that you have lost your early snap and speed;
perfunctory applause is all you earn

and only if you manage to succeed
in going the distance. So, no matter what
they say about experience and the need

for skills that veterans alone have got,
how it gets easier, you know that it does not.

Gray's Allergy

or More Words Overheard in the Students' Bar

'Missed you in The Rose and Crown today.
What happened? On the wagon?
Skint again?'

'I went to Snoopy's seminar on Gray.'

'You what! Old Snoops?
You must be going insane!'

'He told me Thursday, if I didn't show
I'd get the chop.'

'Silly old fart... what did you say
the seminar was on?'

'On Thomas Gray,
his *Elegy* and other boring crap.'

'But that's all medics' garbage, isn't it?
What kind of allergy was it, anyway?
And wasn't Gray the guy who wrote
that big *Anatomy*
you hear the medics banging on about?'

'No. That was Burton, and I didn't say
his "allergy", I said his *Elegy*.
It's famous, or it used to be.
Full of quotes, or so old Snoopy said.'

'Like what?'

'Like paths of glory leading to the grave
and something else about "unhonoured dead".
Oh yeah – here's one that even you would know –
"far from the madding crowd". You heard of that?'

'Some old movie, wasn't it?'

'That's right. And here's another bit...
I wrote it down somewhere... it's really sad...
about these old blokes buried six feet deep...
ah, here it is!
"Each in his narrow cell forever laid
the rude forefathers of the hamlet sleep."'

'That's it?
Can't say I get it.
Who are these four rude fathers then?
RC priests or somebody's dads?
And why's he call them rude? And while we're at it,
how come Hamlet wanders in?'

'You prat! Forefathers as in "ancestors",
and "rude" means – I don't know – just "rough and ready".
Hamlet's a village not a Shakespeare play.'

'All right. No need to get all sniffy.
I'm glad I don't do lit and all that shit
about old buried buggers like your Gray.'

Seldom

is an adverb
I hardly ever use;
very rarely,
almost never.
It's not that I refuse
to choose the word;
it simply doesn't come
naturally to my tongue,
although, to tell the truth,
I rather like it.
Years ago, when young,
I must have decided
for the kind of unreason common in youth
to spike it rather than speak it.
Am I wrong to say
there is something about the word
that is a little spinsterish?
Probably I am.
Perhaps it's more York Minsterish –
the Soho pub I mean,
not the place God put a match to.
Anyway, I don't suppose
you, any more than I,
give a damn,
though what seems odd
is this:
no one I know
has been attracted or repelled
by *seldom*'s adjectival avatar.
Only the poet Spenser,
as far as I'm aware,
made use of *seld*,
a word which, like its meaning,
is indeed rare.

Ambiguities

English is a tongue
rich in ambiguities:
only the other day
I heard an elderly misanthropist,
with both vehemence and acuity, say
'I hate fucking youth!'

'*Youth* must be accusative,' I thought,
'but what of *fucking*?
It could be noun or verb or adjective.'
So in my quest for slippery truth
I asked him what the object was of *hate*.
He said, 'Would you repeat that last remark?'

I attempted to explain I meant no harm
but wished, politely, to investigate
what seemed to me an odd linguistical conundrum;
at which he answered, 'Fuck off mate,'
revealing further strains of ambiguity
but leaving me entirely in the dark.

Famous Guest

Frail yet pungent, gossamer and blue,
Woven by a score of cigarettes,
The light mantilla floats above the stew
Of noise, the restless heads and busy sets
Of teeth and pleasantries. The liquor gleams
And tingling glasses rise and fall in slow
Parody of beating time which wins
As win it must, except perhaps in dreams.

But this is not a dream, the famous guest
Thinks grimly as he stands with fingers round
The warming globe of glass and feels his chest
Grow tight. Soft twangings in his temples sound
As, like a small balloon, a dark yawn swells,
Filling his throat. He swallows it and grins.

Admirers gather round him, all compelled
By sly imperatives they'll later wince
About, remembering their soft surrender,
Saying 'Your last one was magnificent,
Witty, tough, yet curiously tender...'
'I can't think how you manage to invent
Those characters, they're all so different...'
'I love the one you wrote about Stamboul...'
'Another drink, sir? Let me fill your glass.'
He smiles. 'No thank you. Never break my rule –
Not more than three before I dine, unless
I'm safe at home where I can look a fool
With no-one's malice fed or clean dream smeared.'

At last he turns away, still smiling.
This party is a worse grind than he'd feared.
The smoke and noise begin to scratch and sting
His eyes and ears. If only he could sit
And ease the fat fatigue his calves resent.
Yet once he'd dreamed about and yearned for this:
To be raised high, a breathing monument,
Pelted with praise and hosed with adulation;
And this was what he'd feared that he might miss,
This being pumped up taut with acclamation.

A voice jabs disrespectfully and knocks
His thoughts aside. He manages a smile.
The girl's regard is confident, and mocks
Or seems to mock, but lacks deliberate guile.
'Have you by any chance a light?' she says.
And so he flicks the spring and holds the bright
Petal to her face and sees her breath
Draw in her cheeks to shadowed hollows then
Expel the ghost of smoke. She nods her head
Just once in casual thanks. He feels his grin
Still on his mouth and knows it must look dead.

She makes a flippant comment on the guests
And with her ignorant clear eyes defines
His corpulence, the hound eyes he detests
Anew each morning in the bathroom mirror,
His weariness and chronic itch of doubt,
Then turns away and with a thoughtless gesture
The cigarette and he are both stubbed out.

Spy Story

He awoke in a strange bed
In a strange room.
Beyond the grimed window
The street with no name
Was not one he knew
Though he had seen the same
Gaunt features in other places,
The slow and shuffling gait
Of the muffled passers-by,
The faces grey and strained;
The mongrel that sniffed and sidled,
Cocked a leg against a crate:
A stale, anonymous view.
Some of the shops were padlocked.
The windows barred.
He must not linger here
Breathing the alien air,
Smelling old scent and exile.
Stale tobacco and fear.

He descended to the street,
Head down and collar raised
And began to walk towards
The spot where he would meet
His enemy or accomplice,
Assassin or assistant.
Reprieve or last defeat.

He reached the public gardens
And sat on a bench to wait.
The minutes prowled past like prisoners.
It seemed he had come too late,
Or mistaken the rendezvous;
Whatever the error, he knew
His contact was not going to show.
The day began to look older;
There was nowhere else to go.
The bickering wind grew colder
And from the darkening sky,
To rest lightly on head and shoulder,
Came the frail irresolute snow.

The Long Corridors

They are dimly lit by small electric bulbs
concealed high on the walls. The citric light
is unvaried, no matter what the clock might say;
it could be midnight now, sunset or dawn,
or the middle of the day. The rows of closed doors
are as impassive as policeman or palace-guards;
no sound behind them of altercation or chat;
on all of the floors they are identical,
except for the numbers worn on their foreheads
like insignia on soldiers' caps. The corridors
are softly carpeted, collusive with Private Eyes
and smooth adulterers. You may hear the soft whine
of the elevator as it rises or descends,
though no one enters or leaves it, except
for a sullen or shy chambermaid who bears
clean towels for some expected guest or guests.

One day, or night, you may encounter,
soft-footing it along the silent corridor,
someone who inspects the number on each door.
You will not recognise his face, nor he yours,
but of one thing you may be sure: you will meet again,
not in a long, high-ceilinged gallery, but in a place
more intimate, behind a door which he will find,
for he's always had your number and, now, he knows your face.

Epistolary Marriage Counsel

Dear Peter,
                it was good to get your letter
and I'm glad you've found the girl you say will make
the world, and all that's in it, a far better
place to live in.
                    Now, you mustn't take
offence at what I feel I have to say.
Remember I am older and I know
a bit about the games that women play.
I've seen how dew-fresh virgins undergo
amazing changes almost overnight.
A lovely face of guileless innocence
when seen at 10pm in candlelight
can show, at 8am, plain evidence
of petulance, bad temper and a lack
of real intelligence, and furthermore
a sulky whine and raucous squeak and quack
replace what seemed such tuneful tones before.
So promise me you'll come to no decision
about your latest girl, or any other,
before you've undertaken this commission:
make sure you take a long look at her mother,
for there you'll see the shape of things to come.
If, after that, you still decide to marry
I wish you well, although the prospect's glum.
So Mum's the word,
                  Your friend and mentor,
                          Harry.

Dear Harry,
                        many thanks for your advice
which, knowing you to be a wise old guy,
I acted on at once and Paradise
itself has been the consequence. When I,
a little apprehensively it's true,
told Angela I thought it time I met
her mother Angie smiled as if she knew
about your mother-daughter claim or threat.
Anyway, the next weekend we drove
to Sussex where her mother, Isobel,
owns a little house not far from Hove.
Now comes the hardest part of it to tell.
I did just as you said I should: I gazed
at Isobel and she gazed back at me.
The spark of love ignited, flickered, blazed,
and we were both consumed. And so, you see,
your words were wiser than you knew dear Harry.
You'll see the gorgeous creature when you meet her
as you must do very soon before we marry.
Till then I am your most devoted,
                                        Peter.

A La Recherche des Mots Perdus

If I could find my – what-you-m'call it –
my writing-thing,
I'd start a what's-it right away,
but here's the snag, and it's immense:
I see quite clearly what I wish to say,
to celebrate or simply re-create,
but then I am appalled
to find that what the thing is called
is hidden in a haze
impenetrably dense.
Some words that used to come
promptly and obediently to heel
conceal themselves or send
unwanted surrogates
of no relevance or usefulness at all.
For example:
those delightful pretty objects, those
thingummies that smell so pleasant with their red
and velvety soft what-you-call-'ems
would, not so long ago,
have been a perfect subject for – you know –
those little teams of words that can be sung or said.
But what am I to do
when the only way
that I am able to convey
the temper of my thought and feeling is
by using words that once obeyed my will
but now are cruelly concealing who they are
and dancing just beyond my sight and reach
like graceful thingummybobs, those girls
who wear such skimpy little covering-things?
Or what's-their-names – those lovely scented things
I spoke, or tried to speak of, earlier on:
you know – they grow in what's-its
in the open air and people pick them...?

No!... Not winners!... pick with fingers...
Noses?... No!...
What did you say then? Roses? Yes, of course!
To think that I have quite forgotten those,
when I can effortlessly find
words more abstract and more recondite,
like – you know the one I'm thinking of...
Oh shit! It's lurking somewhere in my mind,
yet somehow I can't quite
get the damn thing out and into sight...
It means forgetfulness... sounds like a flower...
You what?... Oh yes, *amnesia*, that's right.

Confiteor

I saw the warnings in my middle years
of penalties survival would impose;
it's paying-up time now – blurred eyes and ears;
scents visit memory but not the nose;
no appetite, except for phantom fare;
this hunger for lost hungers aches and grows;
dead voices whisper on the moonlit stair.

I think I could have prophesied the lot
a quarter of a century ago,
except for this one item I could not
have guessed would shake me like a body-blow,
this need to give a full account of all
the lies and selfish cruelties I know
I have been guilty of, which now appal.

If I could find a way of balancing
the scales with memories of virtuous deeds,
I'd feel less miserable, but rummaging
through those mean treacheries and lusts and greeds
I find no selfless act of charity
or bravery shines there and intercedes,
redressing the account's disparity.

And further searchings turn up nothing more
than flimsy moral negatives to weigh
against the debit side – a dismal score
of unkicked dogs and cats, a dim display
of unbruised babies, unraped girls and boys;
so 'mea culpa' as they used to say,
who prayed that God would mend his damaged toys.

Prodrome

Something terrible is going to happen,
although the world pretends it doesn't know:
an ordinary day, the shops all open,
the usual traffic moving to and fro,
and no one looks more hunted and afraid
than he or she might look on any day.

Music can be heard from open windows,
books are being read, and even written;
lovers saunter through the woods and meadows,
faint smells of cooking drift from hidden kitchens;
swans on the lake glide secretive and slow,
and still the sense of menace seems to grow.

The night arrives like other summer nights;
the music changes tempo, or it dies.
The shops are shut, the thickening dark excites
with whispering scents you can't quite recognise.
Something terrible is going to happen,
permitting no escape or compromise.

Second Thought

However good you are, or think you are,
remember this: there's always someone better.
The smooth guy with the paunch and big cigar
denies it, but the old man in the sweater,
with flattened nose and scars above both eyes,
will nod and grin in rueful affirmation.
You'll take his word for it if you are wise
and be prepared for honeyed adulation,
that comes in floods while you're there, at the top,
to change to sour, derisive hoots and calls
when you're knocked off your perch and forced to swap
punches with old has-beens in small halls.
This is what the young will never know
and maybe it's as well that this is so.

Before Night Falls

There is much to be done
and written and said,
mistakes to be rectified,
words to be read,
before night falls.

But all that you do
spawns more to be done:
if you write to your daughter
you must write to your son;
or make telephone-calls.

Day's jubilant music
already begins
to temper its tempo;
the rich mixture thins,
the eager voice drawls.

Confession, forgiveness,
perhaps time for these:
you recall the old practices?
Down on the knees
with beads or with shawls?

Or draw heavy curtains
and make the lights blaze;
remove all distinctions
between nights and days,
though the silence appals.

However you try
you can't hope to avoid
accounting for all
you have lost or destroyed
within these four walls.

So uncurtain the windows,
and, with luck, that high song
will colour the silence
beyond right and wrong,
before night falls.

Brief Life

an Epitaph

George Gordon, Lord Byron, was one of the best;
he had movie-star looks and was always well-dressed;
a bit of a cripple, but girls didn't care;
he collected their cherries and fine pubic hair.
A versatile player at all kinds of sport
he trained on a diet of beef-steak and port
and gambled for stakes that few could afford.
He had a short innings, but boy! how he scored!

Snow Joke

Some time after midnight it began,
the secretive and silent transformation
of April's variegated score to one
cold and monochrome asseveration
that winter had not yet been overcome.

Next morning's curtains parted to reveal
the street and all its furnishings become,
in their white trance, intransigently still,
each motor car a furry animal,
stunned in hibernation; nameless, dumb.

By nine o'clock no sun to modify
this black and white account of spring's defeat;
the trees in Wharfdale Park were hung with white,
but this was not the metaphoric snow
that Alfred Edward Houseman wrote about.

My dog and I walked over fields that spread
before us like white parchment; feet and paws
inscribed a timeless message with their tread.
I hailed a fellow-walker, asked his views:
'Snow joke!' he called. Or so I thought he said.

Too Late

An evening in late July, still light, although
the sun is being slowly dragged below
the roofs of houses in North Avenue;
these overlook a small but daedal garden;
their slates are dulled and dark, no longer golden,
but the sky remains a tranquil, innocent blue.

The old man gazes through his kitchen window
and listens to the music from his radio,
a fine performance of Strauss's *Don Juan*;
he thinks, unfocusedly, of various things,
of love and music, other summer evenings
such as this; of poetry and Bad Lord Byron.

Evenings like this, except for one great difference:
then he was young, or younger, and in consequence
each day's slow dying was a prelude to adventure,
to the infinitely possible. No longer so;
for, after the sun's cremation, he will know
only a darkness like perpetual winter.

The lingering sunlight and the lengthening shades
advise that it's too late for escapades,
too late for wild nights on the sizzling town,
too late for learning Greek, for reading those
wonderful great books; for growing wise;
too late to go a-roving as the sun goes down.

Knockout

'Counted out, he (the boxer) is counted "dead" – in symbolic mimicry of the sport's ancient tradition in which he would very likely be dead.'
Joyce Carol Oates. *On Boxing*.

He didn't know what hit him. That's a fact,
though now of course he knows it was a fist,
but the knowledge is posterior to the act
and at the time did not indeed exist.

And still, to tell the truth, he doesn't know
which fist it was: it could have been a right,
thrown over his defensive jab, although
a sharp left hook's been known to fuse the light.

The roof fell in and little sparklers waved
and glittered in the dark while both feet fought
about which way to go, and legs behaved
as if to stand was what they'd not been taught.

Next, a senseless page of nothingness,
a neutral tone, not black or white or grey,
immeasurable space of timelessness,
all consciousness completely held at bay.

A little death? If so, with lively hope
of resurrection in most fighters' eyes;
although the phrase can cease to be a trope,
as when poor Johnny Owen failed to rise.

A Serious Bitch

Sally is a serious bitch.
        She never smiles,
but something in those butterscotch eyes
        solemnly beguiles.

The question of her parentage
        remains unsolved,
though a Staffordshire Bull Terrier
        for sure was involved.

She lies, relaxed but vigilant,
        close to my feet,
alert for her next walk or feed,
        or other treat.

I know, and Sally does not, that she
        will die one day:
this knowledge seems unfair, but to whom
        I'm damned if I can say.

Miss Emily

Behind mute walls of secrecy
She hides from peckish eyes –
While from the ivied embassy
Her unseen agents rise.

High and heavenwards they flicker
Above the oblivious town –
Her aerial messengers ride quicker
Than bobolink or sound.

Those tuneful missives are addressed
To God – or certain creatures –
And now – a century gone at least –
They come to tease and please us.

She waits in lamplight – with her Dog –
Until outwearied night
Sneaks away – and through frail fog
Slants epiphanic light.

God and Thomas Hamilton

What falls on the doormat each day is the far
        thunder of wars and the throes
of the horribly wounded and dying, transcribed
        into clichéd mechanical prose;
and televised scenes of the broken and blind
prove starkly what humans will do to their kind.

It is foolish to try to blame God or the stars
        for the anguish and terror we've seen
men causing each other, and then offer prayers
        that divinity should intervene;
but what of those other disasters we name
as 'from natural causes'? For these, who's to blame?

The hurricane, earthquake, the flood and the drought?
        The infanticidal disease?
If God loves his creatures, as Christians maintain,
        how can he give sanction for these?
Not only permit them, but aim from the sky
new ways for his victims to suffer and die?

I presented this question to one who might know –
        a thinker and man of the Church –
who told me the answer would not be revealed
        to those whose crude methods of search
were based on the limited reason of Man,
which would hope to discover an ethical plan.

But God, he assured me, is not of the World,
        His 'thereness' beyond time and space;
His motives and deeds as impenetrable as
        the inscrutable mystery of grace.
Like the actions, I wondered, of him who had slain
those doomed little children that day at Dunblane?

The name, Thomas Hamilton; his smallish arms
      were for culling not cuddling the young;
no one could guess, when he entered the school
      where, shortly before, they had sung
their simple sweet hymns, his revered Smith and Wesson
would be used by its owner to teach them a lesson.

Carpe Diem

How quaint those visions of the future seem,
expressed in verse or, as more likely, prose,
whose source lies not so much in waking dream
as sour distaste for how the present flows,
or fear of new directions it might choose,
as if their authors could divert the stream.

The scenes devised do little to persuade,
like models built from kids' construction-kits,
dated within days of being made;
Utopias, or their dark opposites,
can do no more than flimsy movie-sets
to make us feel more hopeful or afraid.

Those beardless prophets Orwell, Huxley, Wells,
paddled in a future we now see
as concrete history. Our little hells
are much the same dark holes they used to be,
and Eden's gates stay locked. So seize the day,
no matter what the latest seer foretells.

Indian Summer

This day is wholly unsullied,
golden and beneficent. I sit
in my recommissioned deck-chair
by the garden path. From a cerulean sky
the sun's unwinking stare
fixes the world in stasis, warm and somnolent.
This is the weather of myth.
Not a rumour of air
stirs in the limp laburnum, or anywhere;
all is so still and soundless you could hear
the wing-beat of a moth,
except that from my open window drift
faint sounds of Strauss's *Tod und Verklärung*
and yet more faintly, now and then, is heard,
closer, underneath my hand,
dry whisper of a turning page
as I peruse, with awful delectation,
The Oxford Book of Death.

Rope Dance

The last dance of its kind and never again
these morning bells, their cruel carillon
counting the breathings of that young man and woman
who will not kiss, or be kissed by, anyone
ever again. Not that they kissed each other
as lovers, or chastely as sister and brother,
for they did not know one another. And, as they dance,
it's not in graceful tandem in a trance
of silvery sound and with the slinkiness
of Rogers and Astaire, but separate
in time and space, a frisky jig or foot-dance,
kicking and treading frantic air until,
with one last goodbye twitch, their feet are still.

Cocked to one side, each blind and hooded head
seems interrogative, though what might be said
is anybody's guess. Nothing perhaps.
The choreographers in robes and wigs
or starry epaulettes and smart peaked caps
swap slippery grins, though venture no slick answer.
The crowd outside is heard to sigh and murmur,
though not by either motionless rope-dancer.

Castrati

Morning: coffee-breath still staining the air
which carries, too, a contrapuntal sound
drifting from the radio, the strains
of Handel's opera, *Guilio Cesare*.

On Radio 3 of course. Cesto is sung
by a counter-tenor whose crystalline alto,
the presenter announced before the broadcast began,
bears little resemblance to how the old castrati sang.

How would they sound to us, those ancient high warblers –
the famous Farinelli, say? We are told
by learned musicologists their voices
were more powerful than the cool altos of today.

Yet, in imagination's auditorium,
when I try to re-create the sound, I hear
not so much power as a pitiful distress –
a high, waiting cry of inconsolable loss.

Dying Like Flies

'In Chaucer's time, of course,' the speaker says,
'all human lives were cheap. Far more than wars,
the Black Death killed off countless multitudes.
People of all classes died like flies...'

'Like flies?' a somnolescent listener wonders,
and thinks about the fly-deaths he has seen,
remembering those dangling, film-like strips,
glossily slick with toffee-textured glue

and speckled with black and scrunched-up little thorns.
He can't mean those? Or smashed by paper clubs,
quick splat on wall or window-pane? The Plague
never dispatched its victims with one smack.

In Chaucer's time, as now, folk died like folk,
cursing their fate or praying for salvation;
dying, they knew quite well what they were doing.
The fly's way seems the better way of going.

Casualty

Just after 4am he is brought in.
The urgent ambulance that carried him,
and briefly startled sleeping city streets,
delivers its limp cargo and retreats.

A weary charge-nurse says, 'What happened here?'
The paramedic's mouth is skewed and grim:
'Some yobboes out for laughs had too much beer
and kicked the living daylights out of him.'

Kicked the living daylights out of him.
But now the dying nightlights flicker, dim,
before going out, and then the blinds are drawn.

Beyond drained windows birds are heard to sing
by patients as they stir and stretch and yawn.
All taste the waking day, except for him.

A Kind of Glory

in memoriam: Howard Winstone 1939–2000

I

A winter night, the chapel windows bright
with lemon light against the misty dark,
the little houses huddled close for warmth
and mutual protection; you, just twelve,
running down the narrow street, alone,
each breath exhales a spectral bloom, your boots
belabouring the pavement as you pound
your panting way beyond the Workmen's Hall,
past slag-heaps and the pit-gear of the mine
and onward to the hilly countryside:
you're training hard, as grown-up fighters train.

Two nights each week you work-out at the Club,
skipping, groundwork, and the heavy bag,
then, best of all, the sparring in the ring
when all the theory and the fluent moves,
the fantasies of perfect stratagems,
so sweetly economical and swift,
are acted out as sweating fact.
                                        You know
that you will be a champion one day;
you have to be. All of your waking thoughts
are focused on perfection of your art.

Wealth, the noisy worship of the crowd,
might come, but these are never what you crave.
Your love is for one thing itself, the pure
enactment of the perfect moves, a blend
of the aesthetic and the agonistic which,
as spectacle, is thrilling, but to do
is pastime for the Gods, a true vocation.

II

British Schoolboy Champion at your weight
in 1954; then, schooldays ended,
what waited was the factory or the pit.
You chose the factory, though you intended
staying there no longer than the time
it took to reach the statutory age
when you could leave and start the long hard climb
towards the first and necessary stage,
beginning the ascent that every keen
pugilist attempts – a national title.
Your choice proved almost fatal. A machine
snatched and mangled your right hand. Three vital
fingertips snapped off. The shock and pain
were fierce, but far more cruel was the small
explosion of awareness in the brain:
that hand would never make a fist again!

And yet it did, through your determination
not to be denied, although this fist
at first was just a formal imitation
of that destructive weapon you had lost,
and though a measure of its strength returned,
you knew its imperfection permanent.
But your unquenchable ambition burned
more brightly still and it was evident
that you would not surrender. Changed by sheer will,
what seemed to be a vicious trick of fate
became a spur to even greater skill
and speed of rapier left to compensate
for loss of knock-out power in that maimed right.

You then set out to scale the towering hill.

III

Howard Winstone, dedicated fighter,
you did not look the part: too slight, too handsome.
When you, as amateur, were picked to fight
for Wales against the English someone said,
'That boy is far too frail to fight as pro.'
Your trainer, Eddie Thomas, answered him:
'He'll win tonight and when we both decide
it's time for him to turn professional
he'll be World Champion, I promise you.'
And those unlikely words, in time, came true.

IV

The Noble Art, Sweet Science, what you will,
always your vocation, now your trade,
you followed it at home in Ebbw Vale
and Aberdare, the tragic valley towns
you knew and loved so well; then far away,
in London and in Rome, your dazzling skill,
that silvery speed and sleight of feet and hands,
balletic poise and elegance, amazed
and thrilled the crowds no less than your displays
of immeasurable courage and astute
control of each bout's varying demands.
You almost always were victorious
and yet the most consummate exhibition
of your now famous fighting qualities
ended in your dubious defeat.
In 1967, and at your peak,
you fought in Cardiff, fifteen sizzling rounds
against Vincente Saldivar, the great
Mexican whose legend still resounds
wherever fighters meet to celebrate
the heroes of their sport.

That night, beneath
the pitiless candescence of the light
gushing from the lamps above the ring,
you faced the tigerish attacks of one
whose will to win was forged in hammered steel
and met each fierce assault, each hook and swing
and uppercut, with cool and stylish skill.
Your left flashed out, you feinted, sidestepped, swayed
and stabbed again. The dark roar of the crowd
was oceanic, surging in huge waves;
you heard it, not with ears but in the blood.
You foiled the Mexican's belligerence
for thirteen rounds and victory drew close,
but then he smashed through your fatigued defence
and you were on the floor. The crowd's vast voice
was briefly choked and then it was transposed
from exultation to heart-broken woe;
but then it rose again as you, too, rose
to face another onslaught and survive.

The contest ended and the referee
turned towards your corner, then he paused,
and seemed to hesitate; then suddenly
he faced about and moved to Saldivar
and raised the right hand of the Mexican
as winner of the fight. The clamorous roar
of that Welsh multitude was once again
grief-stricken but was seasoned now with rage
as your old friend and handler, Thomas, raved
with anger and frustration. But you shrugged
and crossed the ring to Saldivar and threw
one arm about his shoulders and each hugged
the other wordlessly, survivors both
of one ordeal, co-authors of a true
unwritten epic work to celebrate
pure courage, grace and skill, a kind of love.

V

A hard light, icy, in the corridors
although the air is warm enough; a mix
of smells – distant cooking, laundry scent
and something antiseptic, surgical,
obscurely menacing. White-coated men
and women, preoccupied and serious,
swish on their important business past
slow stretcher-trolleys and their human freight,
one of which is trundled by a short
and stocky grey-haired man of middle age,
his features worn and blurred with weariness,
though there is friendly humour in his eyes.
He wheels his trolley through the swinging doors
to where a male nurse helps him heave his charge
from stretcher on to bed. The porter nods
and says goodnight to nurse and patient, then
he wheels his empty trolley out of sight.
The nurse says to the patient, 'Do you know
who's just now brought you back from being X-rayed?'
'That little porter? No, I've no idea.'
'That was Howard Winstone.'
'Howard who?'
'Winstone the boxer, Champion of the World,
just brought you back and put you into bed.'
'I've never heard of him,' the patient said.

VI

Howard Winstone, Prince among
the finest warriors we have known,
skilful, brave, you stood alone;
but now the final bell has rung.

And all around is heard the sound
of jagged musics and the air
trembles with a chill despair:
nobility lies under ground.

Juggernauts of flesh and bone
lumber round our tarnished rings
launching ponderous prods and swings,
no tune, but tedious monotone.

These clumsy antics are, in part,
gross parodies of what, with skill,
you rang your changes on until
the thing became a work of art.

Old men, it's true, in every age
have claimed the world will never see
again the likes of who might be
the leading player on their stage.

But you were truly nonpareil:
the other tiny giants, Wilde
and 'Peerless' Driscoll both beguiled
and thrilled the crowds, and yet their tale

for sheer enthralment can't quite rise
to that intensity of pitch
of your life's variegated, rich
poem delighting heart and eyes;

an epic narrative that rose
at times in breathless lyric flight,
though ending with the dying light
in bleak and elegiac prose.

And though the splendour of your story
has not been, as it should be, told
and carved in characters of gold,
it still bequeaths a kind of glory.

So let the valleys ring with praise
and gratitude for their brave son
whose every battle, lost or won,
enriched the fabric of our days.

Howard Winstone, Prince among
the finest warriors we have known,
skilful, brave, you stood alone;
but now the final bell has rung.

A Small Epicedium

I am in mourning, though you wouldn't know
from anything I wear that this is so.
It is not possible for me to share
the hurt, nor make it easier to bear
by formalising it in ancient rites
with choristers and priests and acolytes,
for what I mourn is not a long-loved friend
or close relation's lamentable end
but something I alone am broken by,
who didn't think it would ever die:
I mean of course – I wonder if you've guessed –
the tiny talent that I once possessed.

Planning the Occasion

Music and just one poem, not too long,
but something that will pierce right to the bone
and linger in the head. It would be wrong,
I think, to choose a work that's too well-known
or anything too slick and up-to-date:
something by Herbert, or a Shakespeare song,
should strike a note to chime and resonate.

The music, though, is harder still to choose:
it must be something easy on the ear,
yet serious stuff. Not New Orleans blues,
that trails a haze of sex and smoke and beer,
nor anything austere, like late Baroque;
and yet the smooth and richly sensuous ooze
of Suk or Gluck might come across as schlock.

That's not the thing we want, so I must find
a work so lovely it will make them weep
a salt monsoon; don't think I'm being unkind,
for grief of that sort isn't very deep
and holds some spice of pleasure; so I swear
they'll have a ball. That's why I'm not resigned
to not being there, or anywhere at all.

A Place
to Live

Too Late Again

It's late, the daytime voices almost dumb;
the city drowses, drifting close to sleep;
frail echoes of the earlier hum and strum
of human traffic linger on and creep
across the rooftops to this attic lair
in which the weary wanderer lies awake
and listens for the footsteps on the stair
telling him he's made his last mistake.

Too late to make amends, too late to say
that now he understands what those lines mean
which hymn the tender grace of buried day.
The last sounds die but then, quite unforeseen,
he hears the first soft chords from far away:
the wounded music of what might have been.

Something Different

Something different in the air tonight,
not sound or scent, but hints of both of these:
something, or someone, waits just out of sight –
assassin or a terrible disease
about to strike – and yet the moon smiles down
with fat complacency from cloudless skies
on roofs and gardens of the little town,
as if such calm could not be otherwise.

Yet vicious crimes that have not yet occurred
flicker and whisper far away and tease
the eyes and ears before they fade and fall,
until at last no other wound is heard,
only the wind frisking the nervous trees;
no other sound, no other sound at all.

A Place to Live

Gazing down the misty, cobbled years
I recognise that spectral shape, the youth
Hunched beneath his pack of hopes and fears,
Walking the city's streets in search of truth
And, less ambitiously, a place to live
That might with luck be, too, a place to love.

Luck led him into unknown territory,
A room in Chapeltown, a district where
Pale refugees had found a place to be,
If poor, at least alive, breathe liberal air:
The roads were wide, the houses dignified,
Some remnants of a former splendour stayed.

I turn and face the present. Here I stand,
Three decades later, just three streets away:
A little change, some houses gone, the land
Where once they stood is desolate and grey.
The refugees are dark; I hope they find
Clean air of freedom that those others found.

I feel a kinship with most refugees
Though I have found a certain refuge here,
And hope that they have, too. Impartial trees
Of Spencer Place attend another year
Of green display; I trust that they will give
Kind shade to all that choose this place to live.

Blind Corner

A common term that all we motorists know,
yet if we pause to look at it we see
the corner isn't blind: how could it be?
The reason for the caution we should show
as we approach it, carefully and slow,
is not the corner's sightlessness; it's we,
whose eyes, frustrated by geometry,
are blind to danger's nervous stop and go.

The peril, or whatever lurks behind
the corner, drawing ominously near,
might bring us boredom, pleasure or distress;
of course it's possible that we might find
nothing there at all; so should we fear
that nothingness, that blank? The answer's yes.

Last Bus

Suburban midnight,
and the sequinned city
glimmers and simmers
out of hearing and sight,
while here, at the bus-stop,
what's left of November
is a rumour of wood-smoke
and a breeze that can bite.
The solitary man wonders
if he, for much longer,
must wait to escape
from uncordial night.

At last, from a distance,
he hears the slow-swelling
hum of an engine,
then twin light-beams sway
and interrogate darkness
before the last bus follows
and swings round the corner
with its warming display
of bright amber windows;
it looms up towards him,
ignores the lone figure
and rolls on its way.

Love in the Afternoon

The boy and the girl have left their tousled bed
to stroll together in the evening sun.
They love each other, or so they both have said,
and each remembers what was said and done
that day by eloquent limb and nimble tongue,
and he reflects the almost serious fun
they wallowed in is for the lovely young
to relish and the old and ugly to shun.

Ahead of them a man and woman walk
with slow and thoughtful paces. Both are old.
The boy observes that they are holding hands,
like kids or lovers. Neither seems to talk.
The young ones smile and neither understands
that more than hands the old ones, cherishing, hold.

The Story so Far...

An ugly old man is in love with a woman
who is young enough to be his daughter.
She is beautiful, dark and sensuous.
Can it be possible that she returns
something of his passionate devotion and desire?

Common sense, with a shake of the head, says 'No'

but passion might not see or hear this answer.

Occasions do occur when it would seem,
against all odds, she might indeed
reciprocate his love for her,

as when, before the first pale twittering of day,
she turns in sleep, then swimming from its clasp,
draws close to him and draws him near,
holding, sighing and enfolding,
while he grows straight and handsome in the dark.

And are such seemings, then, enough for them?

It seems, without a doubt, they are. So far.

An Ordinary Morning

An ordinary morning in an ordinary summer
of frugal spells of sunshine and a cool
and cautionary breeze saw the old man wait,
thoughtful, on the pavement at the busy corner
where North Parade and Pool Road meet.

A car slowed obediently, then came to a halt
at the paste gems of the traffic lights. He saw at the wheel
a dark-haired young woman; on the rear seat knelt
a boy who gazed out of the window at him
with a stare that showed nothing of whatever he felt.

The woman then turned her head to inspect him
with no more concern than was shown by her son.
Her face was quite pretty but niggling anxieties,
at which he could only guess, had begun
to pencil faint comments around mouth and eyes.

Those eyes that were seeing, if anything there,
an ordinary old man whose life was now over;
no flicker of interest showed on her face.
How could she know he would soon walk towards
the day's white page of illimitable choice?

Mr Kartaphilos

Close to closing-time in Foley's bar –
unshuttered windows smeared with night and rain
two punters sat on stools set well apart
and stared ahead like strangers on a train.

They'd been there for two hours, or maybe more,
and both sipped scotch, and took it nice and slow,
and in the mirror watched at least a score
of other casual drinkers come and go.

At last one very slightly turned his head
towards the silent other: one quick glance,
which slid from real to mirrored face instead,
and then a nod, small, reticent advance.

The other, eyes fixed on the mirror, took
a drink of scotch and nodded briefly too.
There was no hint in either drinker's look
of sexual complicity both knew.

The first man said, 'I know we've never met.
I'm Joe Kartaphilos... Oh, Barman! Same
again for both!... I'd take a fair sized bet
that you don't recognise the foreign name.'

'Can't say I do. You think maybe I should?
It sounds like Greek. Why do you want to know?'
'I didn't think there was much likelihood.
You might have known it, though, long years ago.'

'How long ago? You don't look very old.'
Kartaphilos gave one small grunt of mirth:
'Like someone said, "I could a tale unfold":
truth is, I am the oldest man on earth.'

I am the man that Christ condemned to live
until he came again – the Wandering Jew.'
'You mean you're never going to die? I'd give
a fortune to swap places now with you!'

'That's how they all who hear my tale react:
They think my state is enviable. Not so!
But how can they foresee this steely fact –
that nobody can love you once they know?'

Storm Poem

That night a gale attacked the sycamore,
bullying branches, dashing gouts of rain
in giant fistfuls at the splattered pane,
while in the darkness, warm in bed, secure,
he lay and listened to the swelling roar,
loud in the chimney like an express train,
and longed for sleep to silence it, in vain.
He felt far more awake than hours before.

So he began a poem in his head,
a thing of magic and mesmeric force;
the silver bells of measure swung and shone
and mixed a blend of wit and joy and dread.

Unmarked by him, the tempest ran its course.
He slept. Then woke, and found the poem gone.

Sexy Things

Sexy is the buzz-word now,
Since *buzz-word* has become old hat;
Be careful how you use it though
In print or during casual chat.

The first thing you must understand:
It does not mean what once it meant;
Its referents could not offend
The prudish or the innocent.

It has no link at all with genders,
Nor with erotic stimulants
Like scanty panties or suspenders,
But qualifies Gregorian chants,

Palm-top computers, audio-books,
Certain authentic instruments,
Philosophers and TV cooks,
All found in Sunday Supplements

From which, quite recently, I learn,
With mildest incredulity,
The very latest thing to earn
The 'sexy' tag is chastity.

Good Loser

Joe never even looked the part
    But he could take a punch;
No skill at all, but bags of heart;
    The bravest of the bunch
That used the gym in Fitzroy Square,
He'd take a contest anywhere.

I saw him fight in Leeds Town Hall,
    A kid from Battersea,
Fast welterweight, well-built and tall,
    Who knocked Joe out in three;
But though he took a pasting, Joe
Pleaded for another go.

And less than two weeks later fought
    The same boy over ten
Three-minute rounds at Ellesmere Port
    And got KO'd again,
But this time lasted eight hard rounds
All for a purse of fifteen pounds.

The crowd, who loved him, roared for Joe,
    Although he always lost;
He liked to battle, toe-to-toe;
    Whatever it might cost
In pain, exhaustion, blood and sweat
He gave them what they'd paid to get.

And every time the referee
    Held up the winner's hand,
However bruised, Joe smilingly –
    If he were fit to stand –
Would cross the ring and show each fan
He knew he'd met the better man.

Once or twice he fought a mug,
    A novice or old pro
Who'd work away inside and hug
    And maybe hit him low.
Though Joe appeared to come off best,
The ref, he never seemed impressed.

He'd always pick the other lad
    And Joe would shrug and grin;
You'd almost think that he was glad
    To let his rival win.
We never once saw Joe display
Rage or tantrum, come what may.

He hung the gloves up years ago –
    Not soon enough, we said –
His reflexes and his speech were slow
    From punches to the head.
Last week I saw him in the street,
Shuffling on uncertain feet.

Scar-tissue over both sunk eyes
    That squinted in the sun,
I don't think he could recognise
    Me, or anyone:
Good loser all those times before,
Who might be good for six months more.

The Collector

They are all fine editions,
smart in their original and elegant jackets
which look unworn.

In immaculate rows
they stand, shoulder to shoulder, like guardsmen
parading for inspection.

But they are not inspected,
merely taken down and dusted occasionally.
They have not been read.

They are virginal,
unsmirched by violating hand or eye.
They could be dead.

Their keeper pays
them fairly frequent visits to ensure
that none has got away.

Each time, reassured,
he swallows a necessary and fizzy aperient,
the third one of the day.

In Disguise

The old type sonnet in full fig is out.
Those boys and girls
who, these days, top the bills
at all the most important Festivals,
and often win the coloured prizes,
talk about their 'line-breaks' and such things,
any pair of vocables
that share vague sonic likeness
they will designate as 'rhymes'.
Not for a moment
would any of them undertake
the old gold chimer,
even if they had the know-how and the skills.

Still, all's not lost, maybe.
It might be just
possible to sneak one through the door –
perhaps the Servants Entrance –
in disguise. If not,
then stay at home and wait, and trust
a climate change may yet occur
which could yet restore a taste for shapeliness,
cool argument,
and melody's fulfilment and surprise.

A Kind of Poem

A House of Air,
flowers and warm velvet slippers,
a soft warm blanket for chilly nights;
and – look – a photograph of four young children
dressed as gypsies for a village fete.
A tender memory in a silver frame.
And – listen – what a transcendental sound!
A voice of rich and silken loveliness
embodying the genius of Bach:
a dark red garment for a winter day;
fine printed language waiting to sustain
and yield again its visionary charge
of wisdom and delight.
                          A simple list
of Christmas gifts for yet another year,
all given and received with modest love,
a kind of poem.

Small Mercies

I am waiting for the end
but I would rather go,
not painfully and slow,
but with a sudden bullet
that bursts through the bone balloon,
or high-dive from the summit
of a dizzy-peak to plummet
into the dark below;
yet you and I both know
that I must stay marooned
on this bleak isle of impotence
to wait here for the *Finis*,
grateful for God's providence,
for Schubert and chilled Guinness.

Last
Post

Old

It's not a lot of fun, being old,
nor does it help much when you're told
by well-intentioned friends that you
are something else, not quite untrue,
like 'elderly' or 'getting on'.
On what? I wonder. It must be
the next bus to eternity.
Those who call you 'elderly'
later on are bound to say
'Just heard the news: he's passed away' –
'away' or 'on' – or maybe they
will mention that old so-and-so
has 'popped his clogs', by which they'll show
that they don't give a single toss
for Charon or for Thanatos,
but treat Death with irreverence,
proceeding in the present tense
as if completely unaware
of what the future might prepare
in the way of punctuation –
black full-stop or exclamation
mark that signals all is finished;
not in shape or size diminished,
but over, ended, gone for ever.
Whatever others say, I'll never
play those euphemistic games;
I'd sooner use the simple names
and have it all quite plainly said:
I am old. I'll soon be dead.

Re-reading Sassoon

Something in the mind's dark dug-out wakes,
and images and sounds begin to form;
the shadow and the sound of heavy guns,
their menace muted like a distant storm,
are moving closer as the churned earth shakes
and finally their murderous purpose stuns.

Words, too are heard, coarse khaki verbiage,
their provenance the barrack-room or square;
bleak litanies, nomenclature of things
I thought I had forgotten tread the air,
words of command, prosaic equipage
of butts and boots and packs and rifle-slings.

Our wars, it seems, were similar, and yet
I know the one you fought in was far worse –
the monstrous scale of slaughter made it so –
and though the war I slogged through did rehearse
echoes of that terror, pain and sweat,
it could not be the hell you struggled through.

Yet there was something in the later war
of which we, at the time, were unaware,
dwarfing all the horrors either knew:
the words alone now poison neutral air –
Treblinka, Auschwitz, Dachau, Belsen – more
terrible again, I know, for you.

Black-out

An evening in late autumn, unprepared
to yield completely to the icy steel
of winter's infantry and, in the air,
slight ghost of garden bonfire-smoke still there,
though muffling folds of darkness now conceal
all details of the street in which he waits,
for this is nineteen-forty and a time
when spilling light at night is serious crime,
as German bombers would release their load
of carnage if a splash of glitter showed.

And still he waits, this lad of eighteen years,
and still she does not come. A car slides past,
its headlamps masked, so just the merest smear
of pallid yellow trickles on the road;
and then, as his anxiety swells, he hears
the distant clicking of her heels at last.

This sound is thrilling, more so as she nears.
And now she's here! Her fragrance claims the air;
their lips connect; her closeness sweetly stuns,
although, from far away, deep growl of guns
begins its low and unrelenting threat,
which neither he nor she can hear, as yet.

War Words

I heard the other day of soldiers back
from serving in the fighting in Iraq,
not wounded bodily but suffering from
'post-traumatic stress disorder' – 'bomb
happy's' what they called it in the war
on Hitler; 'shell-shock' in the one before.

And then I thought, Ah yes, I can recall
D-Day, June the sixth in forty-four,
wading through chest-high waves to reach the shore
(the stretch I later learned was called *Sword Beach*,
a place I didn't really wish to reach).
What I that day with many others shared
was '*pre*-traumatic stress disorder', or,
as specialists might say, we were 'shit-scared.'

Still Life

A plum, a pear and a pomegranate
with hard and polished skin announce
their presences on that white plate
resting on the wooden chair
beneath the baffled windows where
a purple curtain softly falls
in sumptuous folds. The bloom of plum,
the yellow-speckled pear and shine
of pomegranate's hint of gold
are unrelated yet aware
of how the dull wood of the chair
is something wholly other than
the otherness of each of them.

Their stillness whispers of a dance
no lilting limbs have yet performed
to music never sung or played,
a seen sonata, tune of shapes,
an unimperilled quietude.

A Word

The shimmering remnants of a summer's day:
a drowsy sun still holds the dark at bay
while, out of sight, a blackbird serenades
his nested mate before the daylight fades;
no other sound until the bells begin
patrolling over fields to reach within
attentive hearts and minds where they can bring
a deeper peace than any bird could sing,
a peace which soothes the torment of the man
who finds, since buoyancy of bells began,
a word, whose sense he does not fully know,
teases with its sound which brings a glow
of gold effulgence in a shadowy place,
an avian shape, and in the air a trace
of heavy scent that moves inside his head
and whispers unheard secrets of the dead.
The word now brings him comfort, soft yet strong:
enough to say it quietly – 'Evensong.'

The Need

I need to make a shape of words,
a singing picture or a prayer,
a declaration of deep love,
of affirmation or despair.

This need has nagged at me for years,
ever since far adolescence,
and now, no less importunate,
it orders total acquiescence.

Though few desires now please and tease –
all passion spent, or stolen by
the pilfering years – this urge to make
sweet verbal music does not die.

So once again I seek a theme
to flesh the spectral shape which might
flower and sing, but what I hear
is 'Try to get the words down right.'

Last Song

for JP

Another day relinquishes
   last memory of sun,
and nightfall prowls the lamplit streets
   as silent as a nun.

I lock the door against the threats
   that populate the dark,
and in my attic room I hear
   a lost dog's distant bark.

Then perfect soundlessness presents
   me with the chance to sing
one small but heartfelt song for you,
   my love, my everything.

I have no wish to trouble you,
   or make you laugh or weep,
but just to sing you one last song
   before I go to sleep.

Last Post

He has written a passionate letter to say
that he wishes he'd spoken these words on the day
that they parted with promises he failed to keep
and he's now being tortured, awake and asleep
by most bitter regrets and frustrated desire
to embrace her again and enjoy the soft fire
of deep mutual longing at last satisfied.
He could never take anyone else for his bride
and his moment of folly must be rectified.
His love for her now has grown deeper and stronger
than ever before and he can't wait much longer
to claim her for his dear beloved forever,
a permanent union none can dissever.

He addresses the letter to where she was living
and trusts it will reach her and stir her forgiving
and generous nature to welcome him back.
He takes the sealed envelope into the black
and wind-ravaged night-time and there asks a pale
and cadaverous stranger where he ought to mail
a significant letter on which must depends,
'You must go,' says the stranger, 'where this lane descends
towards the small village. The place you require
is there on the left and the building is higher
than all of the others. Well, yes, it's a steeple,
and below it, of course, are the deep-sleeping people.'

The Sleepers

Peter, John, Rebecca, Jane,
I softly call your names, then wait.
There's no reply; I call again,
standing by the starlit gate.

Peter, John, Rebecca, Jane,
join me here so we can go
once more along our secret lane
where campions and bluebells grow.

I know it's late, but you will find
the air is mild, the stars are bright;
you need no signal to remind
you where I wait for you tonight.

Peter, John, Rebecca, Jane,
I raise my voice so you are bound
to hear this nominal refrain,
but still no sight of you, nor sound.

And then I see the figure there
in the shadows, hooded, tall.
I feel, but do not see, the stare;
the voice is what I shall recall.

It says 'Hush now, they cannot hear.'
The voice is gentle, dark and deep:
'You won't be meeting them, my dear,
for all of them are fast asleep.'

Safe House

Scent of coffee and the radio's
smoothly laundered voice the listener knows
      will stay completely calm
whatever blood-smeared news it has to bring
to darken this young Sunday in late spring
      with menace and alarm.

And here it comes: a car-bomb in Baghdad
kills forty-three; a sixteen-year-old lad
      shoots woman constable dead;
Keele student raped and strangled in her room;
Russian miners' workplace now their tomb;
      Leeds pensioner stabbed in bed.

The listener's unease soon disappears;
this sun-rinsed kitchen is no place for fears
      of murderous acts or threats.
The radio's voice, unchanged in pitch and tone,
speaks now of some Press Baron overthrown
      and his enormous debts.

He switches off the voice and, gazing out
at that old innocence of sky without
      a cloud in all the blue
framed in his window, finds it hard to see
how such pacific loveliness can be
      co-existent, true.

And later in the morning, when he goes
along his quiet road to church, he knows
      he won't be mugged or shot;
but as he smiles, from somewhere out of sight
he hears the low and ominous growl which might
      be thunder, or might not.

One Man's Music

The poem, the painting, the mosaic of sound –
in one, or all of these things may be found
the source of endless and intense delight,
   yet what might be
   magnificent to me
could seem to you a tedious noise or sight.

We understand that artists must obey
aesthetic rules before they can display
or sing what they have had to undergo,
   but you and I
   are puzzled as to why
our responses to the works should differ so.

The work of art, as far as I can see,
is like its maker who, in turn, must be
one of God's small artefacts, or toys,
   which is why, I suppose –
   as the saying almost goes –
one man's music is another man's noise.

Making Love

That night they made love and it was great;
words in an ephemeral novel, but not
ephemeral words. Made love? But wait –
we catch the obvious sense, but what
is really meant by 'made'? The verb
'to make', with its connotations of 'create'
or simply 'put together', as in bake
a loaf or cake: how can this work
when the delicate abstraction 'love' is 'made'?
If two human bodies meet and unite
in passionate conjunction I rather doubt
that love is 'made' though not, perhaps, locked out.

Love is unique, whether human or divine.
Other emotions such as 'envy' or 'hate',
or the gentler 'joy' or 'hope', may help define
the precious absolute that no one can create
or 'make' but is always there and will wait
to be discovered, though not, I feel,
by grunting couples on a sweaty bed.
But then, just how it is revealed,
and when and where, are anybody's guess.
It might be on the battlefield or playing-field,
in hospital or gaol – or bed? Well, yes:
a flowering of immeasurable tenderness.

Love Rhymes

Rhymes for 'love' are very few
and everyone who ever tried
to write in verse knows this is true.

Search all over, low and wide,
however deep you dig and dip,
just four words settle side-by-side

with 'love' in chiming partnership,
and here they are – I'll put them down:
first 'shove' and 'glove' (both fail to grip

attention whether verb or noun)
while 'dove', 'above', the other two
would make most versifiers frown.

All right. What should the author do,
whose deep desire is to express
how passionate devotion grew

from seed of modest tenderness,
in words that reach into the heart
of her his poem would address?

Well, he must clearly, for a start,
avoid completing any line
with words that would upset his cart

and these 'love' rhymes would undermine
any poet's wish to make
a sweet, melodious word-design.

But who today would undertake
the task of rhyming? Who define
the word itself, now love's dear ache

remains unuttered, as rare wine
stays untasted in the dark,
and what was once the singing line
is now a mad dog's raucous bark?

Missing Things

I'm very old and breathless, tired and lame,
and soon I'll be no more to anyone
than the slowly fading trochee of my name
and shadow of my presence: I'll be gone.
Already I begin to miss the things
I'll leave behind, like this calm evening sun
which seems to smile at how the blackbird sings.

There's something valedictory in the way
my books gaze down on me from where they stand
in disciplined disorder and display
the same goodwill that well-wishers on land
convey to troops who sail away to where
great danger waits. These books will miss the hand
that turned the pages with devoted care.

And there are also places that I miss:
those Paris streets and bars I can't forget,
the scent of caporal and wine and piss;
the pubs in Soho where the poets met;
the Yorkshire moors and Dorset's pebbly coast,
black Leeds, where I was taught love's alphabet,
and this small house that I shall miss the most.

I've lived here for so long it sems to be
a part of what I am, yet I'm aware
that when I've gone it won't remember me
and I, of course, will neither know nor care
since, like the stone of which the house is made,
I'll feel no more than it does light and air.
Then why so sad? And just a bit afraid?

A Few Words to the Not-So-Old

About old age, here's something you might find
worth knowing when senescence's embrace
                    begins to squeeze you tight:
your inability to call to mind
from long ago some once familiar face
                    seems perfectly all right.

It's the things of days, or even hours ago
of which you have no memory at all
                    that cause you some distress;
a splendid poem I thought I'd got to know
by heart would disappear beyond recall
                    within a week or less.

Dates and numbers, names of quite close friends,
even simple words, all fade away
                    before they can embed.
I start a tale, but mislay where it ends.
The lively music I could sing or play
                    lies dead inside my head.

But certain memories will never die:
Tom Fenton's smile, part naughty urchin's
                    grin yet just a little sad,
before the bomb blew it and him star-high
near Mareth as our Company moved in
                    and the universe went mad.

Uncollected
Poems

Nettles

My son aged three fell in the nettle bed
'Bed' seemed a curious name for those green spears,
That regiment of spite behind the shed:
It was no place for rest. With sobs and tears
The boy came seeking comfort and I saw
White blisters beaded on his tender skin.
We soothed him till his pain was not so raw.
At last he offered us a watery grin,
And then I took my hook and honed the blade
And went outside and slashed in fury with it
Till not a nettle in that fierce parade
Stood upright any more. Next task: I lit
A funeral pyre to burn the fallen dead.
But in two weeks the busy sun and rain
Had called up tall recruits behind the shed:
My son would often feel sharp wounds again.

Death of a Snowman

I was awake all night,
Big as a polar bear,
Strong and firm and white.
The tall black hat I wear
Was draped with ermine fur.
I felt so fit and well
Till the world began to stir
And the morning sun swell.
I was tired, began to yawn;
At noon in the humming sun
I caught a severe warm;
My nose began to run.
My hat grew black and fell,
Was followed by my grey head.
There was no funeral bell,
But by tea-time I was dead.

Waiting for the Call

Sitting in the curtained room
Waiting for the distant call,
Hearing only darkness move
Almost noiseless in the hall
Where the telephone is hunched
Like a little cat whose purr
May be wakened if you press
Ear against its plastic fur,
He sits and knows the urgent noise
Probably will not occur:
There's little hope and, if it does,
He's sure – almost – it won't be her.

The Day that Summer Died

From all around the mourners came
The day that summer died,
From hill and valley, field and wood
And lane and mountainside.

They did not come in funeral black
But every mourner chose
Gorgeous colours or soft shades
Of russet, yellow, rose.

Horse chestnut, oak and sycamore
Wore robes of gold and red;
The rowan sported scarlet beads;
No bitter tears were shed.

Although at dusk the mourners heard,
As a small wind softly sighed,
A touch of sadness in the air
The day that summer died.

First Fight

I

Tonight, then, is the night;
Stretched on the massage table,
Wrapped in his robe, he breathes
Liniment and sweat
And tries to close his ears
To the roaring of the crowd,
A murky sea of noise
That bears upon its tide
The frail sound of the bell
And brings the cunning fear
That he might not do well,
Not fear of bodily pain
But that his tight-lipped pride
Might be sent crashing down,
His white ambition slain,
Knocked spinning the glittering crown.
How could his spirit bear
That ignominious fall?
Not hero but a clown
Spurned or scorned by all.
The thought appals, and he
Feels sudden envy for
The roaring crowd outside
And wishes he were there,
Anonymous and safe,
Calm in the tolerant air,
Would almost choose to be
Anywhere but here.

II

The door blares open suddenly,
The room is sluiced with row;
His second says, 'We're on next fight,
We'd better get going now.
You got your gumshield, haven't you?
Just loosen up – that's right –
Don't worry, Boy, you'll be okay
Once you start to fight.'

Out of the dressing room, along
The neutral passage to
The yelling cavern where the ring
Through the haze of blue
Tobacco smoke is whitewashed by
The aching glare of light:
Geometric ropes are stretched as taut
As this boy's nerves are tight.

And now he's in his corner where
He tries to look at ease;
He feels the crowd's sharp eyes as they
Prick and pry and tease;
He hears them murmur like the sea
Or some great dynamo:
They are not hostile yet they wish
To see his lifeblood flow.
His adversary enters now;
The Boy risks one quick glance;
He does not see an enemy
But something there by chance,
Not human even, but a cold
Abstraction to defeat,

A problem to be solved by guile,
Quick hands and knowing feet.
The fighters' names are shouted out;
They leave their corners for
The touch of gloves and brief commands;
The discipline of war.
Back in their corners, stripped of robes,
They hear the bell clang one
Brazen syllable which says
The battle has begun.

III

Bite on gumshield,
Guard held high,
The crowd are silenced,
All sounds die.
Lead with the left,
Again, again;
Watch for the opening,
Feint and then
Hook to the body
But he's blocked it and
Slammed you back
With a fierce right hand.
Hang on grimly,
The fog will clear,
Sweat in your nostrils,
Grease and fear.
You're hurt and staggering,
Shocked to know
that the story's altered:
He's the hero!
But the mist is clearing,
The referee snaps
A rapid warning
And he smartly taps
Your hugging elbow
And then you step back
Ready to counter
The next attack,
But the first round finishes
Without mishap.

You suck in the air
From the towel's skilled flap.
A voice speaks urgently
Close to your ear:
'Keep your left going, Boy,
Stop him getting near.
He wants to get close to you,
So jab him off hard;
When he tries to slip below,
Never mind your guard,
Crack him with a solid right,
Hit him on the chin,
A couple downstairs
And then he'll pack it in.'

Slip in the gumshield
Bite on it hard
Keep him off with your left,
Never drop your guard.
Try a left hook,
But he crosses with a right
Smack on your jaw
And Guy Fawkes' Night
Flashes and dazzles
Inside your skull,
Your knees go bandy
And you almost fall.
Keep the left jabbing,
Move around the ring,
Don't let him catch you with
Another hook or swing.
Keep your left working,
Keep it up high,
Stab it straight and hard,
Again – above the eye.
Sweat in the nostrils,
But nothing now of fear,
You're moving smooth and confident

In comfortable gear.
Jab with the left again,
Quickly move away;
Feint and stab another in,
See him duck and sway.
Now for the pay-off punch,
Smash it hard inside;
It thuds against his jaw, he falls,
Limbs spread wide.
And suddenly you hear the roar,
Hoarse music of the crowd,
Voicing your hot ecstasy,
Triumphant, male and proud.

IV

Now, in the sleepless darkness of his room
The Boy, in bed, remembers. Suddenly
The victory tastes sour. The man he fought
Was not a thing, as lifeless as a broom,
He was a man who hoped and trembled too;
What of him now? What was *he* going through?
And then The Boy bites hard on resolution:
Fighters can't pack pity with their gear,
And yet a bitter taste stays with the notion;
He's forced to swallow down one treacherous tear.
But that's the last. He is a boy no longer;
He is a man, a fighter, such as jeer
At those who make salt beads with melting eyes,
Whatever might cry out, is hurt, or dies.

The Last Fight

This is one you know that you can't win.
You've lost your snap, can't put the punches in
The way you used to, belting till they fell;
You'll have a job to fiddle till the bell.
One round to go; backpedal, feint and weave;
Roll with the punches, make the crowd believe
You've still got something left. Above all, go
The distance, stay there till the end, although –
Even if you clipped him on the chin –
You know that this is one that you can't win.

Lullaby

for Nancy, aged two

The house is silent.
Thick-furred night is heaped against the window,
And one pale, luminous eye remarks
How slowly hours devour the light.
Sleep softly darling;
I shall keep three candles lit beside your bed,
Three golden blades will pierce the heart
Of night till morning finds him dead;
Sleep softly darling, sleep.

For Those Reliefs...

An early morning: the infant school
in Beeston's Nether Street, where Iris White
raised high one hand and called out loudly 'Miss!
Bernard Scannell shit hisself, so who'll
clean up the mess miss?' (Although no fool
she never seemed to get my first name right).
I can't recall what happened after this.
I know that shame was burning on my face
and I could see there was no hope of flight
or any hiding-place from deep disgrace.

I may have been responsible for more
childhood lapses such as Iris saw;
If this is so, I've buried them away
with multitudes of best-forgotten deeds,
but what I'm sure will always stay with me
are later memories from time of war,
not images of carnage, but the way
we lived for months in holes in mud or sand
and had to wait for dark to ease our needs,
as even Iris White might understand.

To leave a slit-trench in the daylight's glare
would be an act of certain suicide
and so, in frequent torture, we stayed there
until, when dark descended, we defied
the snipers' bullets and machine-gun fire,
crept out with paper and entrenching-tools
to leave our dark deposit in the ground,
no laxative required beyond pure fear.
There could have been few areas free of stools
interred by frightened squaddies in that year.

I showed these lines to someone I knew
would judge their merit, giving reasons why
he thought them good or bad, a learned chap.
He read them through with care and then he drew
a deep breath, expelled it with a sigh.
'Won't do,' he said. 'In fact a load of crap.'

Extra Time

He is the star, the one who's bound to score;
For him, the play could run all day or night.
The one the Gods or terraces adore
Has endless stamina and appetite
For worship from the hosts that hunger for
Performance which, as deed and metaphor,
Delivers inspiration and delight.

But what about the walk-on part or role
With three words in Act One and then no more?
Or worse, the striker who has missed the goal
Five times at least and knows he'll never score?
For them the whistle or the curtain-fall
Are sound and sign quite sweet and merciful;
Though what comes next they've never bargained for.

One More Last Poem

One final poem before my pen runs out –
an unconvincing metaphor, I know,
but only one thing's left to write about
and that's the writing game; so here we go,
though once my real, not figurative, pen
is in my hand I find this is not so;
the acts or artefacts of God and men
are what might make the ink or ichor flow.

Love is what first presents itself to me
to place beneath my verbal microscope,
love, which at once reveals itself to be
less sensual than we tend to think, or hope,
and I recall an enviably neat
trope from Wystan Auden that rings true
in which he says should Lust, 'the sapper', meet
with Love 'hug her to death' is what he'd do.

This does not mean that passion's grunt and heave
preclude love's possibility, although
it is a common error to believe
that wild and wordless sexual longings show
the presence of that precious gift which makes
us humans, of all living things, unique;
for love needs language to define its aches
and ecstasies, and we alone can speak.

What next? Well, love and language, it would seem
are treasures that have never lost their shine,
and music's interwoven glint and gleam
and dark deliberations still divine
that otherness which never quite leaves earth,
and though angelic strains might praise or grieve
and hymn the miracles of death and birth
dark silence follows, saying we must leave.

Publishing Vernon Scannell:
Some Personal Memories

The first time I met Vernon Scannell was in September 1962, at the Birmingham Town Hall. At the suggestion of Dannie Abse I'd invited him to join us and several other poets in reading at a poetry and jazz concert I'd organised for the Birmingham Literary Festival. He was a frequent broadcaster in those days, and I knew he had a fine deep reading voice. For Vernon it was a baptism of fire and I recall how quiet and suspicious he was, for jazz was not something he'd encountered before at the many poetry readings he had given, and he was understandably cagey. He looked to me then like a clerk or schoolteacher in his sober grey sports jacket and grey trousers. How wrong first impressions can be!

His reading that day between the musical interludes was powerful and gripping and the enthusiastic response of the large audience quickly put him at his ease. After that first encounter, he soon became a popular regular in these concerts, enjoying the relaxed and lively atmosphere, appreciating the discipline of the music under the skilled direction of the pianist and composer Michael Garrick and the virtuoso brilliance of the other musicians involved. Eventually Garrick set several of Scannell's poems to jazz, including his magnificent Epithets of War, the music perfectly mirroring the poem's various moods and sequences, and Vernon would readily read it with the music whenever there was an opportunity.

At that time I'd just started my own publishing company, Robson Books, and since Vernon was not contractually bound to another publisher, I readily agreed to publish a book of his latest poems. We were all thrilled when that first book for us, *The Loving Game*, became the 'Choice' of the Poetry Book Society, which meant that they purchased a goodly number of copies for their members. We were off to a good start. Over the coming years we were to publish another seven books of Vernon's poems, as well as four volumes of autobiography.

These classic books, which I recommend to anyone who appreciates Scannell's poetry, cover his painful childhood years surviving the brutality of his psychotic father (*Drums of Morning*), the war experiences that were to haunt him and inform some of his finest poems, the period when he boxed professionally and in fairgrounds, and an account (in *A Proper Gentleman*) of the period he spent as poet in residence in the very unpoetic 'new village' of Berinsfield in Oxfordshire, where I visited him. It was then a drab complex of council houses and flats, a few shops, an infant's and a junior school, one pub, and a community centre, which he described as 'an unlettered jungle of red brick, bingo, and booze'. I don't think many poets would have accepted the challenge, often physical and violent, that Vernon faced, for he was not welcome and often taunted by yobs shouting obscenities at him and 'Scannell poet!' He wrote, 'it was as if I were a member of a persecuted minority, a Jew in an anti-Semitic society, a black among racists.' But he stood his ground and eventually won them over, becoming a welcome and convivial regular at the local pub, as I realised when I joined him there!

Not surprisingly, Vernon's reputation as a boxer often preceded him, as it did at Rolle College in Exmouth at a poetry and jazz concert Ted Hughes had helped bring about, and at which he read together with Vernon, Dannie Abse, and myself. In the bar afterwards, a half-tipsy young man tried his very best to provoke Vernon into a fight, but Vernon, showing admirable restraint despite the foul language and insults that were being thrown at him, managed to brush him off. It was a tense few minutes as we waited for fists to fly, but as Dannie Abse said to me later, it was that young man's lucky day!

Vernon was always modest and appreciative, as in a letter he sent me in August 1991: 'In haste. At last I've finished *Drums of Morning*. I hope you find it readable – do you remember looking at the first fifty pages or so and encouraging me to go on with it? Look forward to hearing your thoughts.' Of course I remembered, for I had been eagerly awaiting its completion, and readable it certainly was, compellingly so. I well remember the thrill I felt as I turned the pages of this extraordinarily honest and revealing book, which I thought magnificent, as I hastened to tell him.

If I was lucky and privileged to be Vernon's publisher, I was also lucky to have shared a stage with him for many readings up and down the country over a number of years, sometimes in the most unlikely places. During that period, Vernon often stayed with us in London, and my wife Carole and I also stayed with him and his family at Folly Cottage, his aptly named house in Dorset which he moved to in 1967, writing to me: 'The exiled monarch sends a message to his people: the beer is good, the cider cheap, potent and brutal to the palate, and the girls wear their own complexions and anti-aphrodisiacal maxi-skirts. I ought to do a lot of work here because there's little else to do – unless I take up gardening. The house is fine and at long last I have a study of my own and the children have a big playroom… you must come and see us if ever you can get away for a couple of days. How about it? We could put you both up in reasonable comfort. By the way I have a note in my diary for poetry and jazz in Romford. Are you expecting me?' We certainly were. Then again, three months later he wrote: 'When are you coming to see us… so far I haven't written any nature poetry but once or twice I've felt disturbing symptoms and have even gone so far as to find out the name of a tree in my garden. Yes, I'd like to do the Arts Theatre Cambridge. By the way I see I have a note in my diary for a session at a theatre in Coventry. Is that on?' It was.

How could we resist that visit? Carole and I have vivid memories of strolling with him across the tall fields to the Griffin's Head, where we all drank far too much of the deceptively strong local cider before staggering back as the sun sank behind the surrounding hills. Ironically, it was when Vernon was staying with us that we were burgled. Carole and I had gone out early, leaving Vernon at the top of the house to sleep off a heavy night. It was the intruder's good fortune, given Vernon's boxing prowess, for he heard absolutely nothing, and we returned home to find a rather contrite poet awaiting us, and a number of valued items missing.

Vernon was a great anecdotalist, passionate about poetry, able to complete a *Times* crossword in record time, and full of entertaining stories about his misspent youth and war experiences, which enlivened many a long train journey to this or that town for a reading. He was generous with his knowledge, and drew my attention to many books and poems I didn't know, and also invited me to join him on several BBC broadcasts, particularly for a programme about Thomas Hardy's poetry, a poet he greatly admired. I was to give a 'young' poet's view of his work. Vernon was a marvellous if unorthodox teacher, as Simon Jenkins testified in a revealing *Guardian* article he wrote after Vernon's death. Jenkins (who was later to become editor of the *Evening Standard* and *The Times*, and author a number of books) was ten years old when he attended a school in Hazilwood where Vernon was teaching. 'Scannell was better than a good poet,' he wrote. 'He could teach. It was from him that I learned to love poetry... In the classroom Scannell was a changed man. He did not teach English, which presumably was his job. He simply read poetry from start to finish. He read the entire canon and made us read it back. We didn't have to learn works by heart but he did insist that we recognise by heart what he was reading. This rough diamond of a man would read Marvell's 'To His Coy Mistress' close to tears (from his memoirs I can perhaps tell why). Keats, Wordsworth, Tennyson, Hardy cascaded from the walls. Poetry must always tell a story, he said, but do so by employing metre, scansion and song... his faith in the truthfulness of poetry over all the mediums was boundless.' Jenkins also recalled how Vernon had a boxing ring installed, and taught the boys to box – his other passion.

We shared a number of adventures, including the time we were reading together in Wales over a hot summer weekend. On the Sunday, we found ourselves in a 'dry' county and Vernon was thirsty – very thirsty. It is no secret that he enjoyed his drink, and he lured me into taking a train into the next county so we could test the quality of their beer... returning just in time for the evening reading, which proved rather more spirited than the audience bargained for. Then there was the occasion when we travelled to Hull University with Dannie Abse, a fine poet close to both of us, to take part in a poetry and jazz concert there. Two students turned up in a car to escort us to the venue, one turning to Vernon and saying politely, 'I didn't expect to see you here today, Mr Scannell' (having confused the world war in which Vernon had served). An amused Mr Scannell told him he was happy to be there.

One poem Vernon liked to read was entitled 'Taken in Adultery'... a rather wry and perceptive poem that took an amusing turn on the occasion the actress Betty Mulcahy read it, introducing it in all innocence with the words 'taken in adultery by Vernon Scannell'. Vernon was greatly amused, and I wonder if I imagined the glint in his eye! He was amused too after a poetry and jazz broadcast he'd listened to, sending me this note: 'Heard you on the radio last week with Michael Garrick – very good, I thought. There was a funny moment when Mike said in that rather hushed and reverential voice he sometimes adopts: "and on bass – Coleridge". "My God," said a friend of mine who was listening with me: "Who's on drums and piano, Wordsworth and Hazlitt?"' For the record, the bass player in question was the great Coleridge Goode.

So we often had fun, but there was one particularly dramatic occasion that wasn't fun. In 1987 we published his war memoir *Argument of Kings* and we had arranged for him to be interviewed on a popular BBC radio programme, hosted by the excellent John Dunn, which went out every night at 5pm. Vernon was tickled at the prospect of being interviewed by someone of that name, even if it was spelt differently from that of the poet, and readily agreed to the interview. So powerful was it that, instead of the normal twenty-minute author spot, the producer let the interview run on for nearly an hour, as Vernon talked vividly and movingly to the captivated Dunn about his experiences. A little later Vernon phoned our office to ask what time he had to be at the BBC for the interview. Seemingly traumatised by having visited such deep and troubling experiences, he had absolutely no recollection of having participated in the programme, which was very alarming. Unusually for Vernon, he hadn't touched a drink, and to everyone's relief he wandered into the office a little while later, stone-cold sober.

I should add that those war experiences, apart from the battles themselves, included a time in a military prison in Alexandria when Vernon had deserted after witnessing the consequences of a massacre, but he was given a suspended sentence and went on to take part in the Normandy landings where he was wounded on patrol. While he was convalescing, the war now over, he demobbed himself, but he was eventually arrested in Leeds where he went before a court martial. When he told the judge that he was a poet, the judge queried his sanity and sent him for a psychiatrist's report, after which he was referred to a mental hospital. There a young captain told him, 'This is the last place to get well' and had him discharged within a week. This colourful aspect of Vernon's story came home to roost as we had arranged a launch for *Argument of Kings* at the Imperial War Museum, a few conservative poets and writers, led by Kingsley Amis, protesting at his being given a launch there in view of his history and the book's content. Amis called it 'disgraceful'. It gave the book a good deal of publicity, but the literary director of the museum, a great admirer of Vernon's poetry, stood firm, and we went ahead with the launch, a formidable band of leading poets and writers attending.

It was always a joy when Vernon wrote to say he had a new collection of poems ready, and we would discuss them in detail and together decide on the cover, the blurb, possible quotes we might include on the back, and the promotional possibilities. He was always modest and, unlike some authors, always ready to help. Here is the beginning of a letter he sent in May 1991, just before the publication of *A Time for Fires*: 'After our chat on the telephone the other day, and your mentioning the appalling prospect of my seventieth birthday, it occurred to me that we might try to turn this catastrophe to our advantage.' He then went on to suggest a number of programmes and contacts he thought might be interested. On another occasion, in 1996, when we published *The Black and White Days*, he made a special tape about the book for me to play to our sales reps at a forthcoming sales meeting. It was never easy to get them behind a book of poetry and I thought this might help – and it did. Vernon started the tape by explaining that he'd arrived at the title after a primary school teacher friend of his had told him that when she was talking to the class about her childhood, a young girl had responded, 'Oh the black and white days', presumably because all the films she had seen from that era were in black and white. He then read several of the poems from the book and explained their genesis. Not all the poems, he said, were about the past, though there were several war poems in the book, and not all were 'gloomy', and there were even a couple of poems about the future. He highlighted the poem 'The First Piano on the Moon', the opening poem in this present collection.

His tape brought the book to life in a way I could not have done myself for the reps, who in turn had to convince booksellers to order it, and who had themselves perhaps not read many poems since they were forced to at school, and almost certainly would have never been to a poetry reading. So for them, as for many people, poetry would most likely have been historic and difficult, and hard to sell. But hearing Vernon reading from that book had an electric effect that day, as it had on me now, listening to it again after all these years and hearing that powerful, convincing voice.

The years moved on and sadly the tone of his letters changed as the throat cancer that was to take him began to increase its grip, though his great physical and mental strength kept him writing and going for far longer than expected. In September 1997, I found myself accompanying an author to a literary event in Leeds. I hadn't seen Vernon in far too long, so when the event was over, I took a local train to visit him in Otley where he'd been living for some years.

We sat in the cosy book-lined kitchen of the small grey-brick house he shared with his very caring partner Jo, and we drank beer and talked about old times – the poetry and jazz concerts, the occasions he stayed with us just after our twin daughters were born, the poets we knew, the times we'd shared. We had many memories which Vernon seemed to enjoy recalling, including some of the incidents I've related above, such as the burglary. He showed me photos of himself in the ring, which I'd never seen, and he took down a collection of my own early rough and ready fledgling poems he said he'd been re-reading and asked me to sign it. I was deeply touched. Despite how ill he obviously was, he looked remarkably strong and was as articulate as ever, though his voice was a little hoarse and I felt he was struggling to hide the discomfort, even pain he was suffering – but he was still able to down a pint or two of brown ale.

Vernon seemed genuinely pleased I'd come, and I found it hard to contain my emotion, for we had travelled a long and fruitful road together and he'd enriched my life in many ways. Somehow that visit brought life (and death) into real focus and was a sharp reminder of where its true values lay. I went away with two warmly inscribed volumes of Vernon's more recent poems, and we corresponded regularly until he finally succumbed. His last generous letter to me – a declaration of friendship, really – contained copies of his final brave and moving poems – amongst others, 'Missing Things' and 'One Last Final Poem', which are included here.

It has been a privilege to join with his close friend Martin Reed in putting this final volume together, so that Vernon Scannell's voice may continue to speak to us.

Jeremy Robson

Index of titles